Above there is Heaven, Below there is Hangzhou　上有天堂下有苏杭

LEARNING FROM HANGZHOU

向杭州学习

The story of modern China is composed of over a billion individuals whose destiny has been redirected by unprecedented economic growth and social transformation. The following account of one Hangzhou resident's lifelong experience of displacement helps to set the stage for the rest of this publication in which the larger picture of China's urban metamorphosis is painted.

Sheng Jianhua is a native Hangzhou resident who personifies China's urban and economic climate since 1962. From growing up in factory housing during Mao's era, to living in a luxury high-rise apartment under the modernization efforts of Deng Xiaoping, Sheng Jianhua's life epitomizes the endurance of creating a *xiaokang* society, the term for a middle class of modest means. To this end, Sheng Jianhua has followed his country's path to wealth, albeit without a fixed home. Through a system of continual displacement caused by urban renewal efforts, Sheng Jianhua will have resided in six different homes by 2012. Each of his new homes literally and figuratively advances him to greater heights, from a one-story lane house to a forty floor high-rise, reflecting Hangzhou's rapid pace of construction and zoning facelifts. Although material life has improved dramatically in China, and for Sheng Jianhua, both remain in a state of flux. Like an urban nomad, Sheng Jianhua migrates with his family, shifting with the seasons of demolition and redevelopment, in an ongoing quest for their next shelter.

XIALIN DISTRICT LANE HOUSE

Straddled between China's most notorious political campaigns, The Great Leap Forward (1958-62) and the Cultural Revolution (1966-78), Sheng Jianhua was born into a society that was highly regimented. From the year he was born in 1962 until adulthood, Sheng Jianhua lived with his parents, grandparents and two siblings in a concrete, 1950s era lane house. This thirty square meter government housing unit had a common kitchen facility that the family shared with other workers from the nearby silk, match, and textile factories. At the time, each individual was linked to the infrastructure of the central government through the *danwei* or work-unit system. These organized work groups each had their own housing, schools, health facilities and other public services. The *danwei* monitored all aspects of the worker's life, including everything from housing and food to reproduction. At the time material luxury was renounced and money came in the form of ration tickets to buy basic staples. During an interview, Sheng Jianhua recalls the differences between the past and present:

"In the old times you needed ration tickets to buy different things like rice and meat- even cigarettes. Everything needed a ticket. Each person could only have a certain quantity, for example you were only allowed 0.5 kg of rice per month- it was very strict. But now you can buy anything you want: a car, anything! I'm not saying that we are all very rich, but I'm just talking about the option, a kind of freedom. Back in the old times I couldn't even imagine buying a bicycle. If you wanted to buy a TV for a wedding gift, you had to go through a personal connection. It was an era when everything was controlled."

Amid the height of Mao's legacy, Sheng Jianhua would spend his childhood days in a small elevated room constructed of bamboo that was built into their high ceiling apartment in order to accommodate a growing family. The siblings slept in this room and also used it as a play space where they would convene with friends. Later in Sheng Jianhua's teenage years, the room would be divided with a makeshift curtain in order to give his older brother and wife privacy. Living in close quarters with a shared kitchen enabled daily interactions, and fostered a sense of warmth and intimacy among neighbors. From morning to evening, the families cared for each other's belongings, shared meals and played games that they invented together. What the families could not find in their austere environment they found in their compassion for one another. In this way the families lived free from strife and created life-lasting memories that they would carry with them after parting ways.

XIANLIN SIX STORY

After Mao Zedong died in 1976, China was in a state of uncertainty with no defined political successor. By 1977, Sheng Jianhua and his brother were old enough to work and had joined their mother at the silk factory near their home. That same year, the infamous Gang of Four was detained; signaling the end of the Cultural Revolution.

Former Party General Secretary, Deng Xiaoping who had been living in seclusion, re-emerged as a new leader to become the Chairman of the Communist Party of China in 1978. Deng Xiaoping sought to gradually reform economic policy through the Four Modernizations of: agriculture, industry, science and technology, which fundamentally changed modes of consumption in China. Early reform practices began to permit an emerging sense of individualism from which living conditions became increasingly geared towards more personal space. Consequently, the old house Sheng Jianhua grew up in was demolished to make room for a six-story apartment building, which, at the time, was considered to be a high-rise. Neighboring families and friends were evicted first, disappearing to other districts in Hangzhou. Sheng Jianhua and his brother remained working at the factory and were each allotted one of the newly built apartments. Sheng Jianhua lived with his parents in a forty square meter apartment while his brother lived with his wife in their own thirty square meter apartment. Even though Sheng Jianhua was nostalgic for the solidarity and companionship with his former neighbors, the new space was an improvement, giving him and his parents more room to themselves.

The early 1980s was a time of awakening, when reform practices began gaining momentum. Until then it was as if the entire country had been closed off as a Forbidden City. Known as China's "opening up" to the outside world; the strategy that eventually became implemented is officially referred to as "Socialism with Chinese characteristics". These new policies purported that a market economy and Socialism could co-exist without necessarily being linked to capitalism.

Deng Xiaoping wrote in the People's Daily in 1984 "Socialism means eliminating poverty, pauperism is not Socialism". This principle shifted the nation's focus towards pleasures that had been enjoyed by outsiders for decades. "To get rich is glorious" became the motto for eliminating China's entrenched poverty, initiating a tremendous ideological shift, which redefined the concept of money in China. Sheng Jianhua describes the changing of the times:

"Since then [1978] we started to treat money in a different way. Before, you just used money to buy tickets, but the quantity was controlled so the money didn't mean much. But now we regard money quite differently, money has become more and more important.

After the reform policy our quality of life improved so much. Now we can eat whatever we want, whenever we want, and we can buy whatever we want."

WIFE'S FAMILY FARMHOUSE

In the mid 1980s many factory workers quit their jobs in order to start their own businesses. The silk factory eventually closed down and Sheng Jianhua left for a better salary building highways. He married in 1988 and in 1993 he moved with his wife to her parents' 100 square meter farmhouse located on the edge of Hangzhou. The neighborhood was much like a rural village with mixed-use homes that supported local businesses lining the main road. The ground-level floor of the house was rented out to a restaurant and then afterwards a barbershop.

In 1998 Sheng Jianhua's son was born and the family of five, including the grandparents, lived together on the upper floor. These years of Sheng Jianhua's life were characterized by the first joys of fatherhood and the peace of suburban life. But as Hangzhou expanded and new districts were planned, Sheng Jianhua, once again, became embroiled in the urbanization process. By 2002, the family farmhouse would be demolished. The reason for the demolition was to widen the road upon which the house stood. In the end this new road was never used. Moreover Sheng Jianhua and his family were left without any monetary compensation for their loss.

In China, the government owns all the land but sells, or grants, land-use rights. A family is allowed to build a home on the land, which belongs to them, until the government decides to develop or redevelop the land. When this happens, the land is essentially reclaimed and all houses or structures are removed. Of course, some families refuse to move, prolonging the process until their house is the last one left standing amongst the rubble. Usually these families hold out until they can negotiate a better deal of compensation from the government.

In the end however, everyone living in the development zone loses their home and moves onward to a new location. Sheng Jianhua's farmhouse became a victim of this process. The family was eventually given the rights to a 100 square meter plot of land less than one kilometer away from their demolished home.

SELF-BUILT FARMHOUSE

It was on this plot of land that Sheng Jianhua, using savings and borrowed money, built his new home. This time he made the most of his investment by turning the house into an enterprise. Construction of the new house was completed in 2004 and contained thirteen rooms on four floors. Sheng Jianhua rented out the first floor to a garment factory and housed the workers on the second, while his family and his wife's parents each occupied a floor above the workers. Business was good and life seemed to be finally settling down, until news came that Hangzhou's future downtown hub would be developed on the once peripheral land where his just completed house now stood. The development would be called the Qianjiang New Central Business District and is comprised of local and provincial government headquarters, the Hangzhou National Theater, luxury residential high-rises, international conference centers and shopping malls. In 2007, Sheng Jianhua's home, which stood for less than four years, would be demolished to make way for the future.

As a payment for their sacrifice, the government offered a generous deal to Sheng Jianhua's family. They received a bulk sum of

fifteen million RMB, which more than covers the value of their house. In addition, fifty square meters per family member is reserved for them in one of the newly planned luxury high-rise apartments in the area. Regardless of what current market values will be, Sheng Jianhua's family is guaranteed a future home at a price less than the fifteen million RMB that they were awarded. The only problem is they must wait until 2012 for the construction process to complete.

JIANGGAN DISTRICT APARTMENT

Meanwhile in a remote part of Jianggan District, Sheng Jianhua and his family wait for the completion of their sixth, and hopefully, their last home. "I think this will probably be the last time", he says. When asked if the process exhausts him, Sheng Jianhua states his experiences as a matter of fact: "We're just following the system because we don't have control over it." Reflecting the instability of his physical environment, Sheng Jianhua's career has shifted to that of a freelance driver, using his van to transport people and goods. Yet after all the government administered moves in his life, Sheng Jianhua has actually come out on top. For every year that the family waits, each member is given 800 yuan per month for temporary rent costs. But more than half of this money stays in the bank, earning interest along with the demolition compensation money and situating the family in a more favorable financial position than most.

In 2006, China's economy became the fourth largest in the world. The trajectory of China's growth is illustrated through its physical manifestations and the experiences of its people. The effects of development have provided wealth for many, but its daily psychological toll is a different matter. When asked to recall the home that he is most fond of, Sheng Jianhua returns to the memories of his childhood:

"I like the first house I lived in from my childhood best. It was a good time, and I still think about it because if you are talking about material life, of course things are better now. But, mentally, I think I was happier back then.

The first house was special in that it was safe, because all the neighbors had good relationships. If you were leaving and no one was at home, you didn't even have to shut the door, they would keep an eye on your house for you while you were gone and they would help you no matter what happened.

But now it is quite strange, because everybody shuts the door, often you don't even know your neighbor, and maybe they wouldn't help if anything were to happen. You are more isolated now."

Sheng Jianhua's life parallels the dynamic story of China's past forty-six years. The description of this Hangzhou resident forms a backdrop for the rest of this publication, in which the city's transformative milieu comes alive.

盛建华：杭州游民

克拉瑞萨·迪亚兹

盛建华是一位土生土长的杭州人，从1962年以来经历了中国的城市与经济变迁。毛泽东时代他在工厂宿舍长大，直到邓小平的现代化改革时期才住进豪华的高层公寓，盛建华的生活成为努力创建“小康社会”的缩影，这个术语对于中产阶级来说有着恰当的含义。虽然没有稳定的家，但为了达到这个目标，盛建华追随着自己的国家迈向致富的道路。由于城市重建计划而导致的不断搬迁安置，至2012盛建华住过的住宅类型将达到六种。他的每一个新宅都在进步，从一层平房到四十层大厦，反映了杭州建设和区划的飞速步伐。尽管物质生活在中国发生了巨大改善，可对盛建华来说，却仍然处在不安稳的状态中。就像都市游民一样，盛建华和他的家人不断迁移，随着拆迁和开发周期的变迁，不断寻找着他们下一个栖身之所。

闲林区弄堂中的住宅

盛建华出生在中国最声名狼藉的两次政治运动——大跃进（1958-1962年）和文化大革命（1966-1978年）之间，这时期的社会处于一个高度统一的管理之下。从1962年出生到成年，盛建华一直和父母、祖父母及两个姐弟住在弄堂中一座五十年代的混凝土房子里。全家人生活在政府分配的30平米的住宅中。盛建华周围的家庭来自附近丝绸厂、火柴厂和纺织厂的工人。当时，每个人通过单位与中央政府的基础结构联系在一起。每一个有组织的工作单位都有自己的住房、学校、健康设施以及其他公共服务。工人终身隶属于自己的单位，而单位则监管着从住房、食品到生育的一切事情。因此，物质享受被全然摒弃，金钱以供应券的形式出现，用以购买基本生活用品。在访谈期间，盛建华回忆了过去和现在的差别：

“应该有所发展，因为时代已经在变了。例如，过去你需要用供应券来购买大米、肉甚至香烟这些不同的东西。每样东西都需要一张票。每个人只能定量购买，例如，你每个月只能买1斤大米。那时是很严格的”。

“但是现在，你可以买到想要的任何东西，比如汽车。我并不是说我们都很富有了，而是说可以自由选择。回到过去的年代，我甚至无法想像能买一辆自行车。如果你想要为结婚置办一台电视机，你必须通过熟人的关系。那个时代一切都受到控制”。

在毛泽东时代，盛建华的童年时光是在用竹子搭建的一座小屋中度过的，小屋建在宿舍顶楼上，以便为人口增加的家庭提供足够的居住空间。后来，在盛建华少年时期，这间小屋用一块临时的布帘分开以便让他的哥哥和嫂子有一个私密的空间。分开之前，兄弟俩睡在同一间小屋，这也成了他们会朋友的地方。大家一起生活在公共厨房的小空间里，增进了每天的交流，在邻里之间培养了一种温暖密切的感觉。从早到晚，每个家庭都照料着彼此的财物，一起吃饭，一起娱乐于他们共同创造出来的消遣游戏。简陋环境中缺乏的东西，在他们对彼此的关心当中被找到了。因此，每个家庭免予冲突，也留下了他们后来分开之后，毕生难忘的记忆。

闲林六层住房

在毛泽东1976年逝世之后，中国因为没有明确的政治接班人而前途未卜。1977年，盛建华和他的哥哥到了工作年龄，和他们的母亲一同去家附近的丝绸厂工作。同年，臭名昭著的“四人帮”倒台，代表了文化大革命的结束。一直被隔离的前党总书记邓小平复出，于1978年成为中国共产党的主席。邓小平寻求通过农业、工业、科学和技术的现代化来改革经济政策，从根本上改变了中国的消费模式。早期的改革实践开始允许个人主义意识的抬头，生活条件也开始逐步向更个人化的方向发展。于是，盛建华从小住过的老房子被拆除，为一幢六层公寓让出了空间，他当时觉得这就是高楼大厦。邻居和朋友们首先被赶出去，消失在杭州其他城区里。盛建华和他的哥哥仍然在这家工厂做工，每户分配了一套新建的宿舍。盛建华和他的父母住在一套四十平方米的宿舍里，而他的哥哥则和妻子住在他们自己三十平米的宿舍里。盛建华很怀念过去邻里间的团结友爱，但新的住所毕竟有所改善，让他和父母有了更多自己的空间。

1980年代初是个觉醒期，改革实践开始加速。就好像在此之前，整个国家一直被封闭在紫禁城里一样。最终实现的中国对外开放政策，被官方称为“具有中国特色的社会主义”。这些新政策主张市场经济和社会主义可以并存，不一定必然导致资本主义。

邓小平1984年在人民日报上提出：“社会主义意味着消除贫困，贫困绝不是社会主义”。这一原则使得国家的着眼点转向了几十年来一直只有外国人才能享有的快乐。“致富光荣”成为消除中国根深蒂固的贫穷面貌的座右铭，显示出一种意识形态观点。中国对金钱重新加以界定。盛建华描述当时的那些变化时说：

“从那时（1978年）起，我们开始用不同的方式来对待金钱。以前，你只能用钱买券，但是数量受到了严格控制，所以钱并没有多少意义。但是现在，我们对待钱的态度完全不同了，钱变得越来越重要。”

“改革开放后，我们的生活质量大幅度改善。现在，我们想吃什么、想什么时候吃都可以，而且可以买到任何想要的东西。”

妻子家的农舍

1980年代中期，很多工厂的工人离职，开始下海做生意。丝绸厂最后也关门了，盛建华也离开了那里，为了获得丰厚的工资而去修建公路。他于1988年结婚，1993年他和妻子一同搬到她父母在杭州郊区100平方米的农舍。周围更像是农村，支撑着当地商业的混合式住房散布在大路两旁。这座房子的底层被租给一家餐馆，后来又租给一家理发店。

1998年，盛建华的儿子出生，包括祖父母在内的一家五口人，一同住在顶楼。这些年里，盛建华的生活有着初为人父的喜悦以及乡村生活的平静。但随着杭州扩建和新区的规划，盛建华又一次被卷入到城市化进程当中。2002年，家里的农房要被拆除。拆除的理由是拓宽道路，而房子恰好坐落在道路旁。最终，这条新路未被启用，而盛建华全家在没有拿到任何赔偿金的情况下，被迫迁离。

在中国，政府拥有土地所有权，并出售或批准土地使用权。一个家庭可以在一块土地上建造房屋，房屋属于他们自己，直到政府决定要开发利用这块土地为止。而当这种情况发生时，土地会被收回，所有房屋和建筑物将被拆除。的确，有些家庭拒绝迁出，拖延了搬迁，最后他们的房子成了唯一矗立在碎石瓦砾当中的建筑。通常情况下，这些家庭一直留守到他们与政府协商取得更多的赔偿为止。最后，生活在开发区的每个人都失去了自己的家园，搬到新的地方。盛建华家的农舍也成了这一过程的牺牲品。家人们最终获得了离他们被拆毁的家一公里远的100平方米的土地。

自建农舍

就在这块土地上，盛建华用存款和借来的钱建成了自己的新房子。这次，他做了最大的投入，把房子变成自己的事业。新房于2004年竣工，四层共十三间。盛建华把底层租给了一家服装厂，让工人们住在二层，而他和家人则住在工人上面的楼层。他们的生意兴隆，生活似乎完全稳定下来，但这时有消息传出，杭州未来的市中心将会在一度处于外围的土地上发展起来，而他刚刚建成的房子恰恰就在那里。开发项目将被称为钱江新CBD区，有省市政府部门、杭州国家剧院、豪华住宅大厦、国际会议中心以及购物中心等。2007年，盛建华建成仅四年的房子被拆除，为未来的发展让出空间。政府给盛建华一家人提供了丰厚的条件，以对他们的牺牲作出补偿。他们收到了大约1500万元，作为补偿他们房子的损失。此外，在新规划的豪华高层公寓中将为每个家庭成员保留五十平米的住房。虽然市场价格将来会发生变化，但盛建华一家人被承诺，将来可以用低于他们所得到的1500万来购买这个公寓的房子。而唯一的问题是他们必须要等到2012年施工结束。

江干区公寓

与此同时，在江干区的远郊，盛建华和他的家人正等待着他们第六个住处——有望是最后一处住宅的建成。“我觉得这很可能是最后一次了”，他说道。当被问及这个过程是否令他精疲力竭时，盛建华讲述了自己的经历：“我们只是在顺从体制，因为我们并没有控制权”。反思自己生活环境的不稳定，盛建华改行做了司机，用自己的货车载人和运货。虽然政府管理造成了他生活的变动，但实际上盛建华开始走向成功。每年，这个家庭都在等待着，每位家庭成员每月补贴800元的临时租金。但是这些钱有一大半都存在银行里，和拆迁补偿的钱一起赚取利息，使整个家庭有了比大多数人更好的经济条件。

2006年，中国经济已跃居全球第四。中国发展的轨迹通过国家外在的表现及其百姓的经历充分体现出来。发展已经给很多人带来了财富，而他们每天的心理压力则完全是另一回事。而当被问及他最喜欢的住房时，盛建华回到了儿时的记忆中：

“我喜欢我小时候住过的第一套房子。那是一段美好时光，我至今仍这么认为，因为如果你谈的是物质生活，那么当然现在非常好。但是，从内心来讲，我觉得我过去更快乐”。

“第一套房子很特别，很安全，因为所有邻居的关系都很好。如果你离开，没有人在家，甚至不用锁门，他们在你外出的时候替你看房子，无论发生什么事，他们都会帮你”。

“但是现在就很疏远了，因为每家都锁上门，你甚至常常不认识邻居，也许有事情发生的时候，他们根本不会帮助你。你现在更孤立了”。

盛建华的生活与中国过去四十六年的动荡相呼应。关于这位杭州居民的叙述成为这本书其他部分的背景资料，城市变革的环境在其中生动起来。

LEARNING FROM HANGZHOU 向杭州学习

LEARNING FROM HANGZHOU 向杭州学习

HANGZHOU

The Yangtze River Delta corridor is one of the fastest developing regions in the world. Spanning from Nanjing to Ningbo and encompassing 16 cities with populations larger than 1 million people (with Shanghai, a city of 20 million at the center) the Yangtze River Delta boasts a gross industrial output value equivalent to 21 percent of China's total.[2] It is a region in China that has the most investment, population, environmental pollution and quickest rate of urbanization. The city of Hangzhou, lying 180 kilometers southwest of Shanghai, is a major part of the Yangtze River Delta geographic and economic configuration.

Hangzhou is the capital of Zhejiang province. It covers an area of 16,596 square kilometers and has a population of 7.8 million[3]. In terms of GDP, Hangzhou is the largest economy in Zhejiang.[4] Traditionally known for its beautiful women, rich cultural roots and majestic West Lake, Hangzhou is one of the cradles of Chinese civilization dating back some 4700 years. The famous Venetian explorer, Marco Polo allegedly marveled at Hangzhou's splendor while visiting in the late 13th century calling the city "beyond dispute the finest and the noblest in the world." Today Hangzhou still remains a popular tourist as well as business destination. But while downtown Hangzhou is centered around the picturesque and idyllic West Lake, the backside of the city unravels in a spirit of anarchic ecstasy with no apparent adherence to architectural stylistic integrity or regulations regarding development, size, or signage. Hangzhou's districting efforts have been further confounded by that fact that the city has tripled in size and has seen a population increase averaging over 100,000 per year for the last eighteen years[5]. This free form growth is indicative of many Chinese cities, where city planners cannot keep pace with the accelerated evolution brought on by China's recent economic progress.

SPECTACLE

China's policies of economic reform have not only affected tremendous urban expansion concentrated into a short period of time, including the birth of almost 500 cities since 1978[2], but also yielded an unbridled culture of consumerism. As Deng Xiaoping's reform efforts lifted millions out of abject poverty, a new class system quickly replaced the defective, proletariat model. China's middle and upper classes are growing at such a pace that they are projected to account for 50% of the country's urban population by 2020[3]. In Hangzhou, one of wealthier and more expensive cities in the country, this figure is slightly higher. Newfound wealth has invariably affected consumer choices, consumption rates, and a profound psychological shift in the population.

Emerging from a classless society, in which capital was once considered evil, to an environment that encouraged individual wealth, China has seen millions re-conceptualizing the nature of money itself. It is a scenario that has created a sense of hyper-awareness, where the importance of name brands, quantitative consumption, and individual home ownership now compose the "Chinese Dream". While rapid increases in energy use, natural resources and food have environmentalists projecting nightmare scenarios, opportunistic, multinational companies have flooded China with products and marketing campaigns. Accompanying this new influx of foreign brands is a sense of cultural aspiration and lifestyle advocacy. Growing disposable incomes and cultural changes amongst China's rising classes has had profound ideological, as well as physical effects on the façade of its cities. Manifestations of a new culture of materialism is increasingly evident everywhere: Hangzhou's shopping centers, wholesale districts, advertisement campaigns, fashion trends, housing and cuisine all convey a sense of the insatiable need for more.

The goal of this case study is to index a moment in China's evolutionary transition as it occurs in Hangzhou; to index through an extended visual essay the physical manifestations accrued by economic transition and to examine where sociocultural change and urban development overlap. Furthermore Hangzhou, like every city, is a dynamic organism and many of the trends, objects and phenomena present in the city today are disappearing as quickly as they are established. *Learning from Hangzhou* attempts to record phenomena that will otherwise vanish into the forgotten lineage of China's amnesiac race into the future. It is a project that aims to describe, through photographs, the condition of a civilization and its attendant environment that is alive with frenetic change.

LEARNING FROM ADVERTISEMENTS

This project borrows its title and cue from Robert Venturi, Denise Scott-Brown and Steven Izenour's seminal work, *Learning from Las Vegas*.[2] The authors, in pursuit of understanding the implications of popular culture upon architectural design, observed in a late 1960s Las Vegas that the distinction between architecture and signage was becoming increasingly blurred. Signage, they deemed, was often more important and elaborate than the venues that they advertised, and some buildings were actually signs in themselves. In Las Vegas today this is even more evident with architectural designs that are direct signifiers of the themes and brands they represent: Paris Las Vegas; Luxor Pyramid; New York, NY; The Venetian, etc.

While Hangzhou offers some surrealistic architectural simulacra á la Las Vegas (including a Paris and Venice), it also possesses its own idiosyncratic interrelationships of architecture and signage. These relationships are often confounded by the city's rapid pace of economic and social development. Whereas in Las Vegas, buildings sometimes become the signs, in Hangzhou the constructed environment becomes a stage for the discourse of economic expansion, often leaving architecture at the service of signage. Advertising industries and real estate development, equally prosperous, have in many instances literally obliterated the respective roles of each other. One of this project's main objectives is to investigate how and in what capacity advertising images and structures affect public space, architecture and cognition in general.

Learning from Hangzhou goes on to extend its inquiry of actual signage to the broader spectrum of urban iconography wherein demolition and construction, architectural eclecticism, accrual of habitation, graffiti advertising, climate control and cultural desire all collide in an orgy of semiotic permissiveness that ultimately points to a civilization in the awkward throes of transition.

ARCHIVE

From 2003-2008 I shot thousands of digital photographs throughout Hangzhou based on patterns or visual re-occurrences and then archived them into categories of architectural, socioeconomic and urban cultural phenomena. These photographs cover territory from outdoor advertising, in its many different and all enveloping configurations, to the constructed environment to urban culture's visual codes. Here Hangzhou's transitional zones of demolition/ construction sites, vast architectural stylistic diversity, improvised architectural apparatus', real estate explosion, guerrilla marketing campaigns, internet bars, wedding salons, mannequins and so on have been extracted from the unruly composition of the city and examined individually. It is an attempt to disassemble an urban environment and lay out its component parts. The intention is that by isolating instances of repetition from the overall fabric of the city, processes of urbanization and sociocultural change can be scrutinized more carefully. It is an endeavor to present this developing city codified along the edges of its own physical utterances.

Hangzhou, like most cities, is in a state of constant evolution. Much of the phenomena found in Hangzhou today are disappearing as quickly as they appear. Therefore *Learning from Hangzhou* is a record of the city's last five years (2003 – 2008) of metamorphosis. This dynamic change, most explicit in the transformative effects of demolition and construction, is a situation not only specific to Hangzhou but to all of China. Record growth has tilled China's fields of urban expansion, burying yesterday's relics under tomorrow's imminent hypermodernity. In *Learning from Las Vegas,* the authors cite an architecture that responds to the speed and mobility of America's car culture. *Learning from Hangzhou* is also about speed, a velocity of linear time (the city has tripled in size and gained over a million in population within the last 10 years), and so this project aims to examine the wake that this hurried change has left in its path.

LEARNING

Learning from Hangzhou presents a case study that is representative of transitions happening throughout China; it also provides important lessons for an urbanizing world that is increasingly plagued by a claustrophobic framework of signifiers and frivolous commercialization of public space.

The global market has left an enduring trace of visual clutter on landscapes and cities throughout the world. Turn in any direction today and an advertisement is likely to stare back. But to what degree has this invasion occurred, in what forms, configurations, and in what company have these colorful signs arrived? What other intricate webs of discursive tropes appear in our cloistered urban sprawls? Is there a lexicon of architecture where multiple codes point in all directions at once? What does all this noise mean for our sense of personal space and perception? Answering these questions is the first step to understanding our commercially inundated environment. This project is an indexical answer. Though much of the material presented here may not be novel to readers, in order for its significance to be fully gauged, it must not only be examined in the context of China's own historical, agricultural to late capitalist, trajectory but also in terms of what it means for the future of a global culture.

国家免检产品 中国陶瓷行业名牌产品 国家强制性3C认证产品 设计师信赖陶瓷品牌
嘉俊陶瓷
JIAJUN CERAMICS
旗舰店：杭州陶瓷品市场9厅32-33号（邮局旁）
0571-86082730
馬可波羅磁磚
仿古砖
金舵陶瓷
JINDUO CERAMICS
金牌亚洲
GOLD MEDAL
JIAJUN
嘉俊陶瓷

杭州

长江三角洲是世界上发展速度最快的地区之一。从上海至宁波，包括了16座人口在百万以上的城市（仅处于中心的上海便有一千七百万人口），长江三角洲以工业生产总值约占全国工业生产总值的21%而自豪[2]。这里是中国投资最密集、人口最多、环境污染最严重、城市化速度最快的地区。杭州市座落在上海西南180公里处，(是长三角地区地理和经济格局的一个重要成员)。

杭州是浙江的省会，面积达16596平方公里，人口670万[3]。就GDP而言，杭州在浙江省经济中占据着最重要的地位，自2000年以来，其GDP的年增长率达到13.7%[4]。

杭州自古以来素以美女、深厚的文化底蕴和秀丽的西湖美景著称，可以追溯到4700多年前的中华文明摇篮地之一。据说著名的威尼斯探险家马可・波罗在十三世纪晚期游历杭州时，便为这座城市的美丽惊叹不已，称之"无疑是世界上最精美、最华贵的城市"。今天，杭州依然是深受欢迎的旅游和经商胜地。杭州的中心是风景如画、如诗、如歌的西湖，但城市背后却弥漫着一种无政府主义精神：很明显，它并未遵循建筑风格上的整体性，或在发展规划、规模及标识系统上进行规章管理。杭州当地所做出的各种努力，进一步被这样的事实所困扰：城市规模已增加了三倍，过去十八年来人口每年平均增长超过十万[5]。这种自由形态的增长暗示着很多中国城市的通病：城市规划者们无法与中国近年来经济进步所带来的加速发展保持同步。

景观

中国的经济改革政策,不仅影响了集中在短时期内进行的城市大规模扩张，(这包括自1978以来诞生的近500座城市[6])，而且鼓励着一种肆无忌惮的消费文化。邓小平的改革致力于让千百万人摆脱贫困，而新阶级体系迅速取代了不健全的无产阶级模式。中国的中产阶级和上层阶级也正在以同样的速度不断增长，到2020年将占整个国家城市人口的50%[7]。在作为全国更富庶、更昂贵奢侈城市的杭州，这个数字会更高。新获得的财富无疑影响着消费者选择、消费比例以及城市人口深刻的心理变化。这个曾将物质和金钱视为洪水猛兽的无阶级社会瞬间跃进到一个鼓励个人财富的大环境，使得千百万人重新认识金钱的本质。可想而知，这一切营造出了一种高度的觉醒，名牌、数量消费以及个人住房所有权的重要性成为"中国梦"的主要组成部分。而能源、自然资源和食品的快速消耗，却让专家们仿如遭遇梦魇一般；同时，机会主义跨国公司的产品及促销也涌入中国。与近来这种外国品牌的大量涌入相伴而生的，是一种对文化的渴求和生活方式的倡导。新兴阶级日益增加的存款收入和文化变革，不仅深刻地推动着意识形态的渐变，而且对中国城市的外观有着显而易见的影响。新唯物主义文化的种种表现随处可见。杭州的购物中心、批发站、广告促销、时尚趋势、居室和烹饪都传达着一种难以满足的需求。

本案例研究的目的，在于通过杭州所发生的一切来记录中国发展变革过程中的一瞬间，通过大量的视觉论证，指出经济变革引发的有形表现，审视社会文化变革和城市发展的重合之处。更进一步讲，杭州就像每座城市一样，是一个动态的有机体，里面所呈现的许多流行趋势和现象，刚刚确立起来便会迅速地消失。《向杭州学习》试图记录一些现象，否则这些现象即将被湮灭在中国向超现代奔进的这一健忘的背景当中。该计划目的在于通过照片来描述一种文明现状，以及与其相伴的因狂热变革而充满活力的环境。

向广告学习

本计划的题目和思路，借鉴了罗伯特・文丘里和丹尼斯・斯科特・布朗的力作《向拉斯维加斯学习》[8]。该书作者试图从建筑设计角度来理解流行文化的内涵，在1960年代的拉斯维加斯，注意到建筑与标牌之间的区别变得越来越模糊了。他们认为，标牌往往更为重要，比它们被广而告之的现场更为精美，而一些建筑物本身实际上就是招牌。在今天的拉斯维加斯，这一点在建筑设计上更为明显，它们是所代表的主题和品牌的直接象征：拉斯维加斯巴黎大酒店、卢克索金字塔酒店、纽约酒店以及威尼斯人大酒店等等。

杭州虽然呈现了一些拉斯维加斯的超现实主义建筑幻象，但它也有自身特殊的建筑与标牌的相互关系。这些关系往往受城市经济和社会快速发展步伐的困扰。在拉斯维加斯，建筑有时候成为了招牌，而在杭州，建设环境成为经济扩张演讲的舞台，建筑往往充当了标牌。繁荣兴旺的广告业和房地产开发在很多情形下实际上抹掉了彼此各自的角色。本计划的主要目标之一，就是考察广告影像和构筑物如何以及凭藉何种能力影响公共空间、建筑和普遍的认知。

虽说标牌的无所不在是最初促成这项计划的灵感出处，也构成了其核心要点，但《向杭州学习》更进一步地对广泛的城市景观加以质询。其中拆与建、建筑折衷主义、人口激增、涂鸦广告、气候调节以及文化渴望在符号的过渡纵容当中发生着碰撞，最终指向一种处于转型阵痛中的文化。

档案

从2003年到2008年，根据模式或视觉的再现，我在杭州拍下了几千张数码照片。然后我将这些照片分别归入建筑、社会经济和城市文化现象等类别中。这些照片包括了从多种不同的完全封闭的户外广告，到成为城市文化视觉符码的建设环境。杭州处于转型当中的拆与建的现场、各种迥异的建筑风格、临时的建筑设施、房地产激增、游击式的营销大战、网吧、婚纱影楼、橱窗模特儿等等，均从城市杂乱无章的背景当中被抽取出来，并且个别地予以考察。这是一种分解一个都市环境，并且展示其组成部分的努力，试图通过孤立出反复循环的个案，从而使城市化以及社会文化变革的过程得以更彻底地审视。通过城市自身外观的演绎来展示发展中的城市的一次尝试。

最后，杭州就像大多数城市一样，也处在不断发展的状态之中。今天在杭州所看到的大部分现象，很快就会销声匿迹，就像它们出现时一样。因此，《向杭州学习》只不过是对一个城市过去不断变化的五年（2003–2008年）所作的记录。这种动态的变化，在拆除以及随后的发展所带来的变革效果上是最为明显的，而这不仅是杭州特有的状况，也是中国所有城市的普遍写照。记录发展触及到了中国城市扩张的各个领域，将昨天的遗迹埋葬在明天即将到来的超现代主义之下。在《向拉斯维加斯学习》中，作者引用了一座与美国汽车文化的速度和可移动性相呼应的建筑。而《向杭州学习》也关系到速度，那就是一种线性时间的速率，过去十年内，杭州的城市规模翻了三倍，人口增长超过两百万，审视了杭州这座城市所浓缩的变革在其发展道路上留下的尾迹。

学习

《向杭州学习》展现的是对一个案例的研究，在整个中国发生的变革当中具有代表性，也为一个城市化的世界提供了重要的课题，而这个世界日益被幽闭化的符号以及公共空间轻浮的商品化所困扰。

全球市场在世界各种风景线和城市里都留下了持久的视觉混乱的痕迹。今天，无论你转向任何一个方向，广告都无处不在地盯视着你。但是这种侵犯是以何种程度发生的？以什么形式和外观发生？这些多彩的符号又达到了何种伴生效应？在我们仿若隐居其中的散漫扩张的都市当中，又有其他什么随意附加的复杂结构出现呢？含有代表不同目的的多重代码的建筑是否存在呢？这样的噪音就我们对个人的空间和知觉感受来说有什么意味？回答这些问题，只不过是理解我们这个被（广告图像）淹没的环境迈出的第一步。《向杭州学习》是一个索引式的答案；尽管这里呈现的大部分素材对于读者来说可能并不新颖，但是要使其意义得到充分发挥，不仅必须在中国从农业到资本主义晚期历史性过渡的背景下来考察，而且还要从它对于全球文化的未来究竟意味着什么入手。

水光瀲灩晴方好
山色空濛雨亦奇

从寺庙门口看众神像，每一尊都具有自己的特征 –（缪思的）羊角，（睡神的）沙漏，（希腊女神的）水母，所以信徒能能通过它们辨认众神并且对他们做出正确的祷告。即使建筑没有标牌或指示图，它的样式和在城市规划中所占据的位置也已充分表明了其用途：宫殿、监狱、铸币厂、毕达哥拉斯学校、妓院等。就连商贩们在摊位上摆放商品的价值也不在于物品本身，而在于它们作为其他事物的标志：刺绣的发带，代表高雅；镀金的轿子，代表权力；阿维洛伊的书卷，代表学问；脚镯，代表荒淫。你像翻阅书页一样扫视街道：城市教你去思考一切，使你重复它的论述，而当你确信正游览的就是塔玛拉城时，却不过是在记录她为自己及其各部分所下的定义而已。无论城市的面貌到底怎样，也不管这厚实的标牌之下可能包含或隐藏了什么，你已经一无所获地离开了塔玛拉。

《看不见的城市》– 伊塔罗・卡尔维诺

From the doors of the temples the gods' statues are seen, each portrayed with his attributes—the cornucopia, the hourglass, the medusa—so that the worshiper can recognize them and address his prayers correctly. If a building has no signboard or figure, its very form and the position it occupies in the city's order suffice to indicate its function: the palace, the prison, the mint, the Pythagorean school, the brothel. The wares, too, which the vendors display on their stalls are valuable not in themselves but as signs of other things: the embroidered headband stands for elegance; the gilded palanquin, power; the volumes of Averroes, learning; the ankle bracelet, voluptuousness. Your gaze scans the streets as if they were written pages: the city says everything you must think, makes you repeat her discourse, and while you believe you are visiting Tamara you are only recording the names with which she defines herself and all her parts. However the city may really be, beneath this thick coating of signs, whatever it may contain or conceal, you leave Tamara without having discovered it.

Invisible Cities, Italo Calvino

PART 1:

DEMOLITION
CONSTRUCTION SITE
CYCLES OF REOCCURRENCE
拆与建的重复循环

自1998年以来，长江三角洲地区城市化速度年增长率达到40%[9]。宁沪杭高速公路和铁路以及大运河沿线的九座城市，实际上在共同致力于推进工业产出与投入。2007年的三角洲人口已为九千万[10]。紧随这一扩张之后，便是狂热地改善必要的基础设施，和收获这一增长必然产生的成熟的房地产投资机遇。在杭州，拆迁及随后的施工建设到处可见，并深入到各个公共区域。过时的历史建筑被迅速夷为平地，紧接着矗立起现代化的高楼大厦。

这个过程充斥着整个中国的都市现代化场景。让这台现代化机器二十四小时不断转动的工人们大多是来自农村，到大城市寻求富足生活的农民。这些由农民变成的工人，或民工(一个将农民和工人结合在一起的新字眼）占全国建筑工人的80%（人数达3,200万，大约是加拿大的全国总人口）[11]。这些劳动者负责建设中国光鲜的现代化外观，他们也构成了一个新兴的阶级社会的底层。来到城市后，这些工人的收入可以增加两到三倍，但是他们在经济上仍然没有任何权力，被隔绝于城市社会体系之外。中国城市化的过程预计还将持续二十年，超过五千万农民将汇聚到各个城市，给本来已难以控制的城市人口雪上加霜[12]。仅在杭州，流动的农民工就占城市总人口的10%以上[13]。

中国的城市化进程已经给城市人口结构带来巨大影响和物质变化。有一则笑话说，中国的国鸟应该是起重机。这不过表明“建设”已成为现代中国所处状况的有机组成部分。本书这一章就工地内外的客观表象，考察了拆迁与建设这一循环。

The annual rate of urbanization in the Yangtze River Delta has been consistently well over 40% since 1998.[9] Nine cities along the Nanjing-Shanghai-Hangzhou highway and railway as well as along the Grand Canal have actually joined together in an effort to further boost industrial output and investment. As of 2007 the total population of the Delta was 90 million and growing[10]. In the wake of this expansion there is a frenetic rush to implement the necessary infrastructure and harvest the ripe real estate opportunities that this growth has to offer. In Hangzhou, demolition and subsequent construction is everywhere, often over spilling into public territory. Outdated and often historical edifices are eliminated as quickly as modern ones are erected. It is a cycle where the urban fields of modernization are tilled all over China.

The workforce that keeps this twenty-four hour machine constantly humming consists mainly of farmers who have left the fields in search of a more prosperous life in the big city. These peasants turned laborers or 民工 *mingong* (a new vernacular that combines the characters for peasant and worker) make up 80% of China's construction workforce (32 million people- about the population of Canada).[11] While these laborers are responsible for building China's glossy modern facade they also compose the bottom wrung of a newly classed society. Moving to the city has doubled or tripled these workers' incomes yet they still remain economically disenfranchised and estranged from the urban social system. With urbanization forecasted to last for another 20 years, over a half-billion farmers are expected to swell China's cities adding to an already restive urban demographic.[12] In Hangzhou alone the floating migrant worker population exceeds ten percent of the total population[13].

China's urbanization project is one that has affected tremendous demographic and physical shifts. The joke that China's national bird is the crane is but one of many indications that construction is an integral part of modern China's condition. This section examines the demolition and construction cycle in terms of its physical manifestations both inside and outside the site.

DEMOLITION 拆迁
CYCLES OF REOCCURRENCE
拆与建的重复循环

仿如一种终极牺牲，没有任何怀旧之感地旧建筑便被夷为平地，并为新建筑让出了空间。有时候被画上圈的“拆”字成为指定某些建筑物要被永久拆除的判决标志。在杭州目前恢复重建的过程中，究竟什么是所谓旧的或无用的，似乎完全是异想天开，往往要以安置数千人为代价。虽然被拆除的许多建筑已被荒废了很多年，或缺少必要的设施，但也有一些建成的时间并不久。在中国，建筑的平均寿命只有十到三十年，而世界其他地区则长达七十年[14]。这个统计数字对环境而言意味着灾难，而住在被拆的房屋里的居民，往往被安置在城市偏远区域的那些新建的现代化公寓大楼里。很多人非常高兴地搬迁，有的人却抗拒着这些现代化建筑里相互疏远的生活。而不论怎样，拆迁所遗留下来的都令人联想到战场的残骸，农民们也在这里为中国新兴的回收业收集着废品。

从2004年到2006年，杭州大约130万平方米的建筑被拆除[15]。按照《2008年杭州市政住宅建设规划》，在未来五年内还将拆除500万平方米的建筑[16]。而这些数字同北京相比简直微不足道。按照北京市环保局的说法，2005年至2007年末，750万平方米的建筑已被拆除。假定每人平均生活空间为25平方米的话，这就意味着仅在两年内就拆除了30万人的居所[17]。

With no sense of nostalgia old edifices are eliminated to make room for the new. Sometimes encircled, the character 拆 *chai* (to demolish) is the mark of doom that designates structures for permanent removal. What is considered old and useless in Hangzhou's ongoing process of rejuvenation can seem alarmingly whimsical and often at the expense of displacing thousands of residents. While many buildings demolished are dilapidated or lack proper infrastructure others have not stood for very long. The average life span of a building in China is anywhere between 10 and 30 years, while elsewhere in the world it is upwards of 70 years.[14] While the implications of this statistic spell environmental disaster, the residents of these demolished buildings are often relocated to newly built, modern, high-rise apartments on the outlying areas of the city. Many go happily while others resist the alienating life that these modern structures offer. Either way what is left behind often resembles a war zone where peasants collect the remains for China's burgeoning recycling business.

From 2004-2006 over 1.3 million square meters of buildings were demolished in Hangzhou[15]. According to the 2008 Hangzhou City Housing Construction Plan another 5 million square meters will be demolished in the next five years[16]. These figures are slight in comparison to Beijing. According to the Beijing Environmental Bureau, 7.5 million square meters of buildings have been demolished between 2005 and the end of 2007. If we assume that on average each person has 25 square meters of living space, this means the demolishment of buildings for 300,000 people in just two years. [17]

入口处
110
拆
138
138

进入施工现场
必须戴安全帽

23

拆
138

CONSTRUCTION 建设

CYCLES OF REOCCURRENCE
拆与建的重复循环

一些建筑倒下了，更多的建筑耸立起来。对于建筑设计师而言，中国是他们梦想的地方。到处可以看到正在施工建设的建筑物，而有关建设的统计数字也在不断攀升。根据2004年美国《建筑实录》报道，中国消费了全球生产的54.7%的水泥和36.1%的钢材[18]。而按照国家统计局的数字，建筑行业占全国GDP的6.6%，成为中国第四大行业，截至2005年末，建筑业从业人员有四千万人（大约相当于西班牙全国的人口）。为了跟上杭州城市边界的日益扩张和人口的稳步增长，施工建设在杭州简直无处不在。仅在2007年，杭州市政规划局就批准了12,701,801平方米建筑面积的施工建设[19]。

As buildings come down, even more go up. For architects, China is the land of dreams. Buildings are being built at an alarming rate and the construction statistics tantalize. According to a 2004 report in Architectural Record, the Chinese consume 54.7 percent of the concrete and 36.1 percent of the steel produced in the world[18]. According to the State Statistics Bureau, the construction industry accounts for 6.6% of the national GDP, making it the 4th biggest industry in China and by the end of 2005 there were 40 million people (about the population of Spain) working in the construction industry. To keep up with Hangzhou's expanding boundaries and steadily rising population, construction is happening everywhere in the city. In 2007 alone the Hangzhou Urban Planning Bureau approved the construction of 12,701,801 square meters of building space.[19]

业 的 生 命 安 全 是
中國建築

Large-scale blinds are often erected around the edges of construction sites and wrapped in advertising billboards. These extra large signs (often up to several stories high) are an added structure to the construction site, functioning as both a barrier that protects passersby and a surface that presents an ideal advertising opportunity. This form of signage is particularly relevant to China's rapid cycle of urban development. The construction blind is not only a precursor to the building under construction, and its future role in the market, but also denotative of the social politics of an increasingly classed society. The construction blind replaces the presence of the construction laborer and his second-class status with the promise of consumer goods, often ones that are unaffordable to the worker.

Prematurely erected blinds in areas designated for new construction have created a maze of large-scale ad imagery. These ominous walls, often found along Hangzhou's main shopping strips, are constructs in themselves that help steer civilians to their destination. From the outside the structures appear as an architecture of façade, a completely commodified surface, but the vacancies behind them are often used as parking lots or temporary homes for workers and those who repudiate demolition.

大型遮挡物往往被立在建筑工地四周，被广告牌包裹起来。这些超大的广告牌（往往有几层楼高）是建筑工地附加的设施，既充当着防止路人进入的屏障，也是承载又一个广告机遇的平台。这种形式的广告牌尤其同中国城市发展的快速循环关联在一起。建筑遮挡物不仅预示了施工中的建筑物及其未来在市场上的定位，而且显出了日益等级化的社会的社会政策。建筑遮挡物取代了建筑工人的存在及其边缘地位，而它承诺的商品往往是工人们负担不起的。

在某些地方为新的建设项目而过早地竖起遮挡物，形成了由大型广告牌组成的迷宫。这些充满不祥之感的围墙往往在杭州主要购物街区都可以看到，它们构成了广告迷宫中的通道。从外面看，这些设施是完全二维平面的建筑，非常商业化的表面，但是它们后面的空地却被用作停车场，或民工和那些反抗拆迁的人们的临时住所。

THE BILLBOARD AS BLIND
作为遮挡物的广告牌
拆与建的重复循环 CYCLES OF REOCCURRENCE

电话：（86）57
传真：（86）57

建筑三局
浙江中南

四两"博"千金 丰厚回报等您拿
www
网狗在线
GOD PARENT
100万
青春寶
美容
胶囊
家家e易家
定制 短信
08.10.24
MAX歌友會
熱力無
戈雅 西
真情理财
SINCERE FINANCING
九龙大道一号
翔桥514路公交车直达
具系列
BOSCH
进口
买
杭州农副产品
现代 浙江
执法
认真
■经营卷烟必须领
■零售经营户必须
■运输烟草专卖
中国建筑服务跨越五
创建绿色
州湾的明珠
肉制品系列
中华人民共和国国境口岸认证

7月6日—8月31日
宋城
泼水
咨询电话 8008571233
易文传媒
肯德基
花都
超越时尚
REN
心动演唱会
快乐香港游
看台统一票价: 280元
"台湾食品城"进驻浙江食品市场
招商热线 88750028 88750038
太湖源頭
Be ture,Be yourself.

莱依
看我的
夏雨

鳳凰城，精裝亮相。
高级城市公寓
酒店/酒店式公寓
甲级纯写字楼
风尚商业街
精装修样板房已对外开放，欢迎光临现场品鉴。
现场售楼处 ← PHOENIX PLAZA

西 W.
仁和路
东 E.
Renhe Rd.

世界
动12580
喜，等你来拿！

看
浙江经视

WORKER HOUSING 工人宿舍

CYCLES OF REOCCURRENCE

拆与建的重复循环

工人宿舍往往是用蓝色塑料表层的聚苯乙烯泡沫墙面或厚混凝土板制成的，已成为一种无处不在的建筑形式，随着中国的经济发展和城市化进程而涌现出来。

建筑工人或民工（转入建筑行业的农民）承担着建设中国现代化外观的任务。这个不断迁移的群体构成了中国流动人口的绝大多数，始终栖息在建筑工地的那这些标准化、可拆式的宿舍里。这些高度实用化的设施通常每个房间能容纳12人，配有一个建在旁边的公共洗浴设施和食堂。尽管对于雇主来说，这些栖息地十分方便而且廉价，但是民工们却被有组织地阻搁于城市生活之外。他们被限定在建筑工地里，生活在一个终日充斥着噪音和灰尘的环境中。一旦一座建筑物建设完工，一个工人的工作也就告终，他们的住所和游牧般的生活便又重新开始。因为建筑业的工作并不短缺，工人的艰难历程通常还包括搬迁到下一个建筑工地去。

The worker dormitory, often made of blue, plastic coated Styrofoam walls or thin concrete slabs, has become a ubiquitous form of architecture that has emerged alongside China's economic development and urbanization efforts.

Construction workers, or 民工 *mingong* (farmers turned construction workers) are responsible for erecting China's facade of modernity. This transient group, which makes up the majority of China's floating population, is almost always housed on the construction site itself in standardized, portable, dormitory style buildings. These highly utilitarian constructs usually house up to 12 people per room with a public bathroom facility and canteen located nearby. While these homes are convenient and inexpensive for the employer, the *mingong* are systematically prevented from integrating into city life. They instead are confined to the site, living in an environment of constant noise and dirt. Once a building is complete and a worker's job ends, so does their residency and nomadic life begins again. Since there is no shortage of construction work the worker's trek usually involves moving directly to the next construction site.

路体育中心工程
创文明城市让天更
571-85455050 85453098
公德

鼎力雕刻机

P

宝业建设
东方金座
40-100平方米
精装修小户型

tel:87701688
瑞立·

·中央花城
FLOWER CITY

程 树 萧 宏
60

好 美 的

GREAT GREEN WEB 大绿网

CYCLES OF REOCCURRENCE
拆与建的重复循环

挂上帘子的脚手架、帐幔、陷阱、包装、保护物。在建筑工地上，一片片绿色织物点缀着杭州市，看似森林中的树木。人造绿网常常是挂在用作施工围帐的竹竿或金属脚手架上。正如艺术家克里斯托，他将著名文化纪念碑包裹起来，是为了重现它们；这些绿网神秘地遮挡了具体细节，反而夸大了未来建筑物的构架。绿网还安全地接住掉落下来的物体、泥土、尘埃和工人。建筑物的完全显露通常是在瞬间发生的。就像围巾从头上被重新戴在脖子上一样，高耸的建筑物外表一旦装饰完毕，几层楼的绿网立刻就被揭去了。往往在不经意间，另一个光鲜的新建筑便进入了城市景观之中。

Draped scaffolding, veils, entrapment, packaging, protection. Along with the multitude of construction sites, pockets of green drapery pepper the Hangzhou skyline like trees in a forest. Sheaths of synthetic green webbing usually attached to bamboo or metal scaffolding cloaks partially formed constructs. Similar to the artist, Christo wrapping significant cultural monuments in effort to re-display them, these green webs mysteriously cloak the specifics and exaggerate the edges of the edifice to come. The green webbing also safely contains falling objects, dirt, dust and the worker within. A building's unveiling usually happens incrementally and quickly. Like a scarf being readjusted upon the neck, several stories of green webbing are undraped at once to unveil a newly mounted curtain wall. Often unnoticed, another glossy new erection swiftly enters the cityscape.

95598

中国联合代建
浙江宝业

发挥党员作用
争创先锋工程
努力拼搏奉献
确保「双优」工程
江南监理

限公司

杭
州
二

SOYEA

万通房产

保 安 全

请您戴好安全帽
亲人盼您安全归
安全责任重于泰山

PICTURES OF PLACES TO COME 未来图景

CYCLES OF REOCCURRENCE 拆与建的重复循环

在建筑工地及城市的其他地方，开发商们借助充满诗意又打动人心的妙语和计算机绘制的产品形象，来为自己生产的商品做广告。无论是用于豪华公寓、购物中心还是写字楼，这些未来的人物和地点的图景被描绘得生动真实，那些想象中的居民、客户和场景都非常理想化。华丽的词藻也常常被用来描述西方人、豪华汽车和知名时尚品牌。看着施工过程努力接近其蓝图，而有时两者互相紧邻，让人有一种异常强烈的似曾相识之感。

在北京，这些广告最近已引发了争议，市委市政府谴责它们破坏了建设和谐社会的目标[20]。使用“超豪华”、“至尊”、“极端舒适”和“享乐”这类字眼来赞美豪华住宅，这些广告被认为是疏远了大多数城市居民，因为他们无力负担如此昂贵的住宅。在一个所谓的社会主义国家里，这些广告刻意迎合那些渴望有别于老百姓的人们，显得有些矛盾。据滨江房产集团的一位代表说，购买一处豪华房产就意味着巩固了客户较高的社会地位和权威。

在杭州，新公寓地产的竞争是极为激烈的，广告牌并非是为新开发项目作宣传的唯一手段。其中还涉及到一场媒体的赤膊战：在报纸、飞机杂志和奢侈生活杂志、电视上刊登广告；付费的新闻报道以及各种公共营销活动，都被用来增强对顾客的吸引力。但是大部分客户是因为“口碑”——这种传统的方式来作出选择[21]。

In front of most construction sites and elsewhere in the city, developers advertise their goods through poetic catch phrases and computer renditions of their product in the making. Whether it is for luxury apartment complexes, shopping malls or office buildings, these pictures of people and places to come are hauntingly realistic, even idealistic, with imagined residents, clientele and scenarios. Portrayals of Westerners, expensive cars and trendy name brands frequently figure into these illustrations' grand narratives. Watching the construction process strive towards its imagined, completed condition, sometimes right next to its illustrated version, elicits a surreal sense of déjà vu.

Recently in Beijing these advertisements became a source of controversy when the mayor and local government accused them of undermining the goal of building a harmonious society.[20] Extolling the virtues of deluxe accommodation by using such terms as “supreme luxury”, “utmost prestige”, “extreme comfort”, and “hedonism” the advertisements were thought to alienate the majority of the city's citizens who are unable to afford these expensive apartments. It is paradoxical that in a so-called Socialist State these ads cater specifically to those who aspire to distinguish themselves from the masses. According to representatives of Hangzhou's Binjiang Real Estate Group, buying a luxury property is meant to reinforce the client's high social status and sense of importance.

Competition for new apartment complexes is fierce and billboards aren't the only means of advertising new developments in Hangzhou. A full-fledged media blitz including: ads in newspapers; in airplane and luxury lifestyle magazines, on television; paid for news articles and public marketing events are used for building visibility and attracting customers. However most clients come the old fashion way-by word of mouth.[21]

发
更优雅。
广东发展银行
文明
之上
The Upper Class.
城之恋
区核心、杭州一流
中心庭院建筑
滨江生活样板
景江城市花园
住宅和SOHO
巩固发展创卫成果
齐心同育文明
杭州四建市房产档案馆工程

等待
让我们
11月11日
湘湖人家
浙江省中医院

效果图

PART 2:

ARCHITECTURAL ECLECTICISM STYLISTIC DIVERSITY PAST & PRESENT
建筑折衷主义
风格多样化，过去与现在

杭州是中华文明的摇篮地之一。早在4700多年前，人类就在该地区建立了“良渚文化”[22]。2200多年前，中国的第一位皇帝秦始皇把杭州设为郡[23]。自那时以来，利润颇丰的丝绸和茶叶贸易以及持续不断的行政捐税，奠定了杭州作为一个文化中心的地位。毋庸置疑，杭州的建筑历史是丰富而多样化的。很多古建筑多年来或毁于政治斗争或年代久远，但也有少数被修复，成为旅游景点。这些“古典”建筑，连同杭州的西方殖民主义和社会主义的现代史，以及当今多元化的后现代主义时代，给整个城市留下了各种风格并存的现状。按照西湖区的一位城市规划者的说法，这座城市有着它自己独特的建筑流派，即“杭派”，也就是当地学界传统的现代风格[24]。也有人主张，当地建筑的特色并不在于市中心文人雅士的居所或学堂，而是市郊那些富于想象力和高度风格化的农舍。本章考察的就是杭州建筑风格中强烈的折衷主义。

Hangzhou is one of the cradles of Chinese civilization. 4700 years ago humans established what was known as "Liangzhu Culture" in the area.[22] 2500 years later China's first emperor, Qin Shi Huang established it as a county.[23] Since then the profitable silk and tea trade along with continued political benevolence has contributed to Hangzhou's status as a cultural center. Hangzhou's architectural history, needless to say, is also very rich and varied. While many of its ancient buildings have been destroyed by political strife or age over the years, a few have been recently recreated as tourist sites. These "classical" structures along with Hangzhou's modern history of Western colonialism, Socialism, and now, the pluralistic era of postmodernity have left a potpourri of styles throughout the city. According to one of the West Lake District's city planners, the city also has its own school of architecture, the *Hangzhou School* 杭派, which is a modernistic stylization of the local literati tradition.[24] Others may argue that local architectural distinction is found, not in the elite residences and academies of the city's center, but in the imaginative, highly stylized farmhouses on the outskirts. This section examines the robust stylistic eclecticism of Hangzhou's architecture.

CLASSICAL 古典式样

ARCHITECTURAL ECLECTICISM

建筑折衷主义风格多样化过去与现在

杭州丰富的文化和政治遗产，及其有史以来一直是中国富庶地区的地位，共同给这座城市留下了无数的古典建筑风格。宋、明、清各朝建筑与中国最古老的清真寺、罗马天主教堂共处其间，杭州也有因为在19世纪和20世纪初欧洲资本家在此落户而留下的种种建筑。在浙江大学，遗留下来的苏联式建筑不禁令人想到中国曾经是自己北方近邻亲密的共产主义伙伴。今天，很多标志性建筑都被视为古典风格，包括雷锋塔和城隍阁，均是对原建筑进行了改造，增添了新的设施，例如电梯和钢架结构。这种对古建筑的模仿再现，有助于保持杭州的古典风格，对其旅游业也至关重要。

Hangzhou's rich cultural and political heritage mixed with its status as one of China's more traditionally wealthy areas has left the city with a myriad of classic architectural styles. Song, Ming and Qing dynasty structures share space with one of China's oldest mosques, Roman Catholic churches, and what's left behind of Hangzhou's legacy as a home to European capitalists in the nineteenth and early twentieth centuries. In Zhejiang University, remnants of Soviet style Socialist architecture are a reminder of China's not so distant communist courtship with its northern neighbor. Today many monuments considered as classical, including Leifeng Pagoda and Cheng Huang Pavilion, are reconstructed versions of the originals with new amenities such as elevators and steel structures. These simulated renditions of antiquity help Hangzhou maintain the classical allure so crucial to its tourist industry.

建设生活品质之城
功德坊

湖山信美

義源

麦当劳

優の良品
AJICHIBAN

CHINESE MODERNISM 中国式现代主义

ARCHITECTURAL ECLECTICISM

建筑折衷主义风格多样化过去与现在

“一种形式一旦被置于某种文化语境之中，便属于那种文化了”[25]。这句话引自建筑大师保罗·安德鲁（Paul Andreu），就中国土地上大量充斥的由外国人设计的建筑而言，它可以用来充分说明中国作为一个国家和一个民族所具有的强大适应能力。不论外国建筑大师的设计多么异质，但由于现实的建筑改造和使用，或者仅仅因为中国势不可挡的文化环境，于是不可避免地变得中国化了。但在外国建筑师更加符号化的影响下，我认为中国存在着一个本土特有的现代主义分支，它也是形成杭州目前城市景观的重要组成部分。这是一种以宏大而率直，有时高度精美的方式，清楚地体现纯粹形式的设计模式。这些风格当中，有些可以在有大型立柱或圆角处理的建筑中看到。政府建筑为了突出政府的权威，也采用了一种独特的、形式化的设计思想。这些建筑物要么是对国际化风格引发的现代主义传统的松散解读，要么就是当今全球各种建筑风尚融合而成的一个自己的门类。

“A form, once placed in a cultural context, belongs to that culture”[25]. This quote from architect Paul Andreu exemplifies the enormous adaptive capacity that China as a nation and as a people have had on the plethora of foreigner-designed architecture in their country. No matter how foreign the designs of foreign architects may appear they inevitably become Sino-fied by either the more tangible conditions of construction, modification and use, or simply by China's overwhelming cultural context. However, amidst the more iconic influences of foreign architects, there is a brand of modernism that I have identified as particularly indigenous to China; and one that has helped to shape Hangzhou's cityscape. It is a mode of design that articulates pure forms in heroic, candid or sometimes flamboyant ways. Some of these trends can be seen in buildings that include a large column or curved cornered treatment. Governmental buildings, with their evocation of power, also employ a unique, formal design strategy. Whether these buildings are loose interpretations of the modernist legacy initiated by the Internationalist Style or recent amalgamations of global architectural trends they have constituted a category in itself.

注浙大首届才子才女大赛

CHINESE MODERNISM
GOVERNMENT BUILDINGS
政府建筑

There is a brand of Chinese Modernism that is chiefly employed for government buildings. While these structures can come in a variety of styles, each has a stout, symphonic, and often imposing presence that touts the brazen power and authority for which the People's Republic is known. According to one joint-venture firm, government bids are not necessarily reserved for Chinese architects but they do, however, carry a list of unwritten rules that belong to the Confucian tradition. Many of these rules are intuitive or learned from examining existing government buildings. Before winning their current bid for a government complex in Hangzhou's industrial sector of Xiaoshan, advice was given that "the most important politician's office should be the biggest; higher than everyone else's; and have the best view"[28] Other unspoken criteria involves: imposing elevations- something that might have trickled down from Stalinist architectural influences; a good sense of both symmetry and *fengshui*[29]; and broad expanses in front of the building should be left empty to reinforce the notion of power. While design fees are modest for these projects the building fees are potentially limitless, "they simply want it to be great".[30]

中国现代主义的另一个类型，便是政府建筑。尽管这些建筑可能风格各异，但每一个都有坚固、和谐、并且往往外观宏伟，突出表现人民共和国的权力与威严。按照一家合资企业的说法，政府招标并非只认准中国建筑设计师，而是遵守着一系列从属于儒家传统的不成文规则。其中很多规则是凭直觉形成的，或者是通过考察现有的政府建筑而学来的。在最近一次为杭州萧山工业区政府大楼竞标之前，就有人建议："重要领导的办公场所应该是最大的，要高于其他建筑，还应有最好的视野"[28]。另外一些不成文的标准包括：令人难忘的雄伟壮观，这也许是斯大林式建筑影响的遗风；良好的对称感和风水[29]；建筑物正面的开阔地应该是空旷的，以强化那种权威性。尽管这些项目的设计费是有限的，但建设费潜在地说却是无限制的，"他们只想要'大'"[30]。

CHINESE MODERNISM

ROUNDED FRONT

圆形设计

Wandering in the city of Hangzhou a pattern emerges of buildings that are shaped like an L where the elbow is pronounced by a flat, angled panel or an enlarged, rounded column. Usually situated at an intersection, with the building's main entrance stationed at the pivot point, two wings flank out in either direction to straddle the entire corner. These buildings usually house banks, business offices, hotels and the like. While there is no willing acknowledgement of this specific design mode as a learned style, the Hangzhou architect, Wang Shu hypothesized that the rounded front buildings are most likely the products of Tongji University graduates who might have misinterpreted the Japanese Metabolists who were considered trendy in China during the Eighties.[26]

"In the early 1980s, Japanese architecture had a great impact on China. It was not long after the opening up policy, books were rarely available and most people could not read foreign languages. However, Japanese magazines were half written in Chinese characters, and some were figured out through guessing. China was heavily influenced by the Japanese Metabolic style of the 1950s. It was a school of architecture that produced many fantastical buildings, for instance, large cylindrical forms as affixes, or a city expanding into space, ocean or the universe, etc. It was influential at that time because it was modern, and utopian. But when it was realized in China, it just became a common building with a spiral staircase."[27]

在杭州这座城市里漫步，会发现一种建筑模式，外形仿如字母"L"，用带拐角的平面或大型圆立柱来突出的"肘"型。这种建筑通常坐落在十字路口，建筑的入口位于中间，两翼向外延伸，横跨整个街角。进驻这些建筑的通常是银行、商务办公室、酒店等等。没有人愿意承认这些特殊的设计模式是一种舶来品。而杭州的建筑设计师王澍提出，这种圆形外观的建筑很可能是同济大学毕业生们的作品，它们可能曲解了八十年代一度在中国流行的日本新陈代谢派[26]。

"中间其实有一段时间是受日本的影响很大，就是在八十年代初。那时候我们刚刚开放，可以看到的书很少，尤其是我们的外文又都不好，日本的杂志因为有一半是中文，猜猜也能大概猜得出来，它的书寄来得很多。那时候受日本50年代的新陈代谢派的影响，比如一个建筑旁片放一个圆筒楼梯，这实际上是一个典型的50年代日本幻想中的超级城市。新陈代谢派当时做了很多幻想型的建筑，比如说大的圆筒，像插件一样，城市向空中、向海上、向宇宙中蔓延等等，做过很多那样的。那个对中国当时的建筑有影响，当时很现代啊，它是乌托邦。到了这儿的痕迹就变成一个普通的板楼边上加了一个圆的楼梯筒，就是这种做法。但这个是在80年代初很短的一段时间，就过去了"[27]。

POSTMODERNISM, IDENTITY CRISIS
后现代主义身份认同危机
ARCHITECTURAL ECLECTICISM
建筑折衷主义风格多样化过去与现在

通常认为，建筑中的后现代是用“谐趣、装饰和参照”的回归而预示的[31]。建筑理论家查理斯·詹克斯则发现，后现代主义本身并不单单是一场运动，而是一系列“不连续的运动”共同促成了各种不同风格的大融合[32]。这些定义不仅反映了杭州的城市景观，而且也反映了构成这一景观的诸多因素。一位游客曾用同样是五花八门、纷杂热闹的中国大餐，来比喻这座城市就是一道建筑大杂烩。虽然这种多元性常常造就了丰富多彩的结果，但也反映了某种身份认同危机——这一点在后现代原则的参考文献中被重点强调。在中国目前的建设浪潮中，设计师们不仅挪用了罗马、希腊以及殖民时期的建筑样式，而且还创造性地让这些风格奇特地融合。

It is generally thought that Postmodernity in architecture is heralded by the return of “wit, ornament and reference”.[31] The architectural theorist, Charles Jencks finds that postmodernism isn’t a movement per se but a series of ‘discontinuous movements’ that amount to a conglomeration of styles working in different directions.[32] These definitions reflect not only Hangzhou’s cityscape, but also many of the individual components that comprise it. One visitor, referring to China’s miscellaneous and often messy communal meal, alluded to the city as an architectural *hotpot*. While this plurality has often produced quite colorful results it also reflects a certain identity crisis - one that can be found in the emphatic concentration on the reference part of the postmodern tenet. In China’s recent construction boom designers have not only appropriated Roman, Greek, and colonial modes of architecture, but have invented curious amalgamations of these styles as well.

杭州宋城
ALEPHAN GROUP CO.,LTD.
ALEPHAN HOTEL

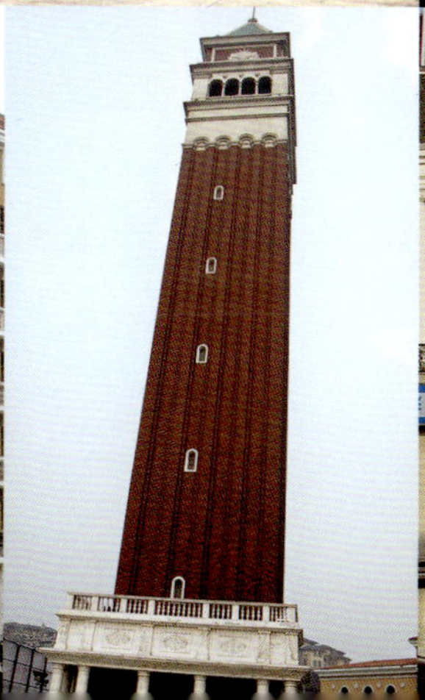

POSTMODERNISM
WESTERNISM
西方主义

While western classical motifs in architecture and interior design had once signified opulence and sophistication for China's nouveau-riche it has quickly become mainstream and can be found virtually everywhere. Greek columns are now more frequently seen than the coiled eaves of traditional Chinese architecture. This exoticism of western classical styles is something that one real estate agent noted was a way to flaunt one's sense of internationalism.[33] Not all appropriated styles are blatant (Hangzhou has its own housing complex renditions of Venice and Paris), some are subtler and more urbane, e.g. colonial lines imbued with a modernist elegance in apartment complexes or the pervasive borrowing from classical Art Deco designs. Art Deco motifs have had considerable influence on Hangzhou's new architecture, which in the city's closest neighbor, Shanghai, is ubiquitous in its original form. Like the Gilded Age from which Art Deco emerged, appropriated styles today still resonate loudly for a culture that is currently looking out more than it is looking in.

对于中国的新兴暴发户来说，建筑和内装设计方面的西方古典基调一度意味着富裕和精美，它很快便成为主流，随处都在运用。现在希腊式立柱往往比中国传统建筑的卷檐更常见。一位房地产经纪人提到，这种西方古典风格的异国情调是炫耀一个人的国际化意识的手段[33]。并非所有挪用来的风格都是庸俗的，有些更为微妙精致，更为都市化，例如公寓大厦中渗透的高雅的现代殖民风格的影子，或者高度借用古典装饰艺术风格（Art Deco）的设计。装饰艺术风格的基调对杭州的新建筑有着相当大的影响，在毗邻杭州的另一座城市上海，这种风格的原型随处可见。就像镀金时代涌现出的装饰艺术风格一样，今天挪用来的风格对于目前这个向外看而非向内看的文化而言，产生了更大的共鸣。

英皇鐘錶珠寶
EMPE ROR

POSTMODERNISM

CHINA STYLE VS. HANGZHOU SCHOOL

后现代中国风格对抗杭派

In Tan Kok-Meng's *The Big Shift*, the Shanghai based architect poses the question: How to be contemporary while still being Chinese? The answer to this question is often found in what he calls *China Style*, a quick fix towards identity[34]. This manifests itself in traditional motifs being hoisted upon modern structures with varying degrees of success. Sometimes it is seen in a simple capping of a building with what resembles the sweeping gable roof of traditional Chinese architecture. Elsewhere it can be found as a fully integrated system of materials and spatial design in what has been identified by Zhang Jianming, a city planner for the West Lake District, as the 'Hangzhou School'. From his observations this style relies on Hangzhou's literati and artistic tradition as well as the city's relaxed, natural surroundings for inspiration. "The Hangzhou School encompasses the utilitarian space of Western modern architecture with cultural elements attached on the surface. It has a welcoming and relaxing characteristic without any solemnity. Simply put, the Hangzhou School has restored the utilitarian functionality of architecture, and uses materials found in proximity to nature." According to Zhang, the Chinese Academy of Art, which sits on the edge of the West Lake, is a good, albeit magnified example of the Hangzhou School, while the academy's new campus in the outlying suburb of Xiangshan, designed by architect Wang Shu, is a an example of the Hangzhou School gone awry.[35] While Wang Shu himself would deny the existence of such a School, his designs are marked by a clever, even radical synthesis of traditional and modern. [36]

在谭克蒙（Tan Kok-Meng）的《大转折》一文中，这位在上海生活和工作的建筑设计师提出了这样的问题：如何在保持中国特色的同时，与当前时代合拍？对这个问题的回答，往往是用他所说的“中国风格”，这一解决身份问题的即时修正[34]。这一点，从不同程度上，在强调传统基调的现代建筑中，成功地得以表现。有时候可以在建筑物简单的屋顶设计中看出来，如类似中国传统建筑物中广泛运用的人字形屋顶。在其他地方，也可以被视为一个综合的材料和空间设计体系，被西湖区城市规划设计师章建明称作“杭派”。据他观察，这种风格的灵感来自杭州的学界和艺术传统，以及这座城市闲逸的自然环境。“就是既有现代建筑的使用空间，又在外观造型上体现中国的文化元素，同时也融合了一些西方的现代元素在里面，这个特点让人们感到很亲切，很轻松，不会特别严肃，很简单，“杭派”建筑是回复到建筑本身的实用功能上，用的材料都很贴近自然”。按照张建明的说法，坐落在西子湖畔的中国美术学院就是杭派稍有夸张的精彩典范，而由建筑设计师王澍设计的地处象山远郊的新校区则是杭派的变体[35]。尽管王澍本人否认这一派别的存在，但他的设计明显地带有巧妙综合传统与现代的痕迹[36]。

9

INTERVIEW: ARCHITECT, WANG SHU
建筑师王澍访谈摘录

Wang Shu has been called one of the most experimental and outspoken architects of China. Born in 1963, he surprised the world at the 2006 Venice Architectural Biennale with the Chinese contribution "Tiles Garden: A Dialogue Beyond City, Between an Architect and an Artist". Wang Shu is founder and currently director of Amateur Architecture Studio as well as Professor and Head of the Architecture Department at the China Academy of Art, Hangzhou.

Below, Wang Shu discusses his long-term relationship with Hangzhou, its architecture, and some of his own endeavors including his collaboration with his partner Lu Wenyu on the mesmerizing China Academy of Art, Xiaoshan Campus.

"I came to Hangzhou in 1988 and hung around until 1995 when I moved to Shanghai (for graduate studies at Tongji University). Then I came back again in 2000. I have been here since. At the time, Hangzhou was still nice and very relaxing. One could still walk from one end of Nanshan Road to the other with your eyes closed without having to worry about being run over. There were fewer cars and fewer people. The place was peaceful until 2002, but in 2003 it suddenly changed into this. It was a typical urban transformation. Now, as a professor of architecture, I often tell my students that it's hard to recall any calm state of being, and, as a result, the students are unable to produce anything that has a calming effect since they haven't experienced what calmness is to begin with.

People have often described Hangzhou as "Heaven on Earth". The highlight in Hangzhou is still its lake and restful surroundings. Coupled with this lake would be the original households, which are infused with the scenery. Unfortunately those houses are almost all demolished. It would be difficult to imagine what type of city Hangzhou once was. A few days ago, a friend was reminiscing about his childhood, recalling each household, its walls, gates, water pond, fish tank, and the few people who lived together in one courtyard. In the 1950s, after liberation, Hangzhou housed a population of two hundred thousand. One can imagine a very beautiful city with a population of only two hundred thousand! Those large courtyards must have been tranquil occupied by only a few people.

Initially there was a plan to preserve this. The president of China Architects Association, decided the dimensions of all buildings should be made in accordance with Baoshu mountain. In other words, buildings should not exceed it. The first to break this rule was the Wanghu Hotel. Today we see Wanghu Hotel only as a seven to eight-story building, but at the time the building provoked a great debate and opinions varied. However the one building that really marked a decisive change in Hangzhou was Xinqiao Hotel, the first high rise in Hangzhou, which fundamentally subverted the rules - a remarkable 18 floors, 50 meter high building. Once it was built, it firmly stood up along Yan'an Rd changing the entire scale of the area, since the city was not supposed to be seen from Su causeway of the West Lake. Once these buildings were constructed, the overall urban landscape changed. All of this took place in the late 1980s.

In fact, a lot of Chinese cities including Hangzhou once had the opportunity to choose, yet most of them did not adopt the approach of building a new city while preserving the old one."

Mathieu:
Since your return in 2000, what are your insights into architecture here? Besides your academic tasks, what other kinds of projects have you worked on?

Wang Shu:
Early on there were very few architectural projects, and I focused instead on interior design and renovation, which I considered an excellent way to practice. Our school had also set up a design company. Working there allowed me to be in contact with the first group of nouveau riche in town. At the time, besides cab drivers, small restaurant owners were among the first to become wealthy. They had little education, but they were audacious enough to venture out on their own and open small clothing stores, restaurants, drive cabs.

They were actually the first to accept some of my interesting ideas. Due to the competitive atmosphere, everyone was always renovating, so I wanted to do something different. The more unique the better, although what I proposed was not outrageous, just very unique. I remember they even accepted the proposal I had for a small Karaoke place. The client wanted to turn it into a small theatre. This motivated me a lot, but they had a small budget. So I came up with the idea of only using wood —identically sized wooden blocks that were to be nailed onto the entire space. I decided on a plan, drafted a drawing and showed it to the workers. I told them that for the next 24 hours, they were to nail the blocks in a haphazard, improvised pattern, like an explosion. The overall effect resembled a blown up piece of wood. It was inconceivable to the workers that renovation could be done like this.

Mathieu:
As the city expands outward and advances, what challenges, opportunities, and responsibilities do contemporary architects and educators face? What do you tell your students since there are so many opportunities now?

Wang Shu:
First of all, as a contemporary architect confronted with such circumstances, one should have a sense of social responsibility. One should be conscientious. For instance, it's a pity some ancient buildings are demolished. Our lives have become restless, however, we should realize that we live in a unique era. A century ago, the earth was only populated with 1.6 billion people, and now it is nearly 7 billion, something that is unprecedented historically. This is especially significant in China.

What I've been working on mostly in the past two years has been combating waste by recycling abandoned materials from other demolition sites for new buildings. If you visit our Xiangshan campus you will notice a lot of the newly constructed buildings are made out of recycled materials. For the front half, we used more than 3 million pieces of recycled materials including old tiles, bricks and stones. People were astonished to see a facility of such caliber made with large quantities of recycled materials in China.

I have a strong sense of time. As traces of time appears on an object, I find it extremely beautiful. The current approach seems to try to catch up with time, but in fact it is working against time. It abandons the old, while new objects have yet to be marked with time. They are brand new, which has made me skeptical about them. Life should be inclusive, for instance we have memories that are old. One has wishes and dreams, but also memories, which makes one whole. If one is absent of memories, and when memories become fictional, just like those Qing dynasty TV episodes, wouldn't it be scary?

In traditional Chinese houses there was a way of life to be followed, a cultural concept that included family, ancestral, or Buddhist rituals. These elements formed certain patterns. Family now consists of two parents with a child. The social structure has been dissolved, thus past traditions cannot be inherited. It is indeed an interesting era. At the same time, it's a critical era. Is it possible to reconstruct a meaningful lifestyle projected through architecture, and could architects ever achieve this? Vice versa, you can also imagine a certain type of architecture that would have an influence on society. Take a residential complex developed by a real estate company for example. It might not be what we would like it to be, but it does directly reflect our current way of living. Those tiny units can be a big headache for the designers because the client requests that each unit is small while independent, facing north or south, with a good amount of natural light and ventilation. Those requirements pose challenges, while at the same time they reflect how society has reintegrated itself and its values.

For example, I designed a residential building in Hangzhou as an experiment. It's a 100m residential high-rise located at the end of Qiantang River Bridge at Qianjiang. Each unit has a two level courtyard, which gives the impression that no matter which floor you live on, you would always feel that you live in a duplex. Secondly I wanted to make it possible for people to plant trees even at 100m above the ground. A regular balcony is normally 1.5m deep while mine is 3m, which is rather deep. This form manipulates the balcony space, thus you would think it's a house instead of being a balcony.

Houses have begun to transform without having a comprehensive solution ready in hand. While many would think of it as chaotic, it is an interesting era. It can also be thought of as a fortunate time, because in this process you could make certain things that would impact an era of living.

王澍被称为中国最具实验性和最坦率的建筑师之一。 生于1963年，他的作品《瓦园——一位建筑师与一位艺术家关于超越城市的对话》作为2006年威尼斯双年展国际建筑展中国馆的唯一作品，引起了全世界的关注 。 王澍当前是业余建筑工作室的创建人并且是杭州中国美术学院建筑系的教授兼主任。

以下是王澍关于他长期以来与杭州的关系，它的建筑，和他自己的一些努力，包括他与陆文宇在迷人的中国美术学院象山校园的合作的讨论。

“我到杭州是1988年，在杭州混了几年，95年去的上海，2000年又回到杭州，一直呆到现在。当时我觉得杭州还是挺好的，特别放松。当时我记得那条南山路上，你可以闭着眼睛从马路这边走到马路那边，不会有车撞倒你，非常少的车，人也很少，非常安静，是那样一个地方，南山路一直到02年还是那个样子，突然从03年就变成那样了，就是非常典型的城市的变化，因为当时曾是为这个事苦恼，就是西湖边上旅游，背山路那条线是很热的，称为北线，南边那条线按道理也有很多可看的，但永远热闹不起来，非常的安静，大家就会认为安静是件坏事儿，一定要把它变得不安静。但我倒很不习惯，我喜欢原来的样子。因为我现在当老师了，教建筑，我经常跟学生说，因为大家现在在这个处境里，基本上已经忘记了曾经有一种生活可是非常非常安静，学生现在做安静的东西他也不会做，因为他完全不知道了什么是安静了。

杭州实际上我觉得，像这么一个地方，我经常说，以前人们说杭州是像天堂一样的一个地方。但是杭州原来最好的是这个湖，完了边上就是特别放松，它是一个跟这个湖结合得很好的，就是我们以前说的民宅，其实杭州的民宅才是原来最好的一个东西，和风景能够融合在一起，那么今天我们看到的杭州，最大的缺憾就是这种民宅基本上全部被拆掉了。曾经杭州是一个怎么样的城市，已经很难想象了。我们学校前两天一个朋友还在那儿回忆，他的童年就是这样的，一户一户进去，一道墙一道墙，一个门一个门进去，水池，金鱼缸，一个大院子里不住几个人，因为杭州城在50年解放的时候，是20万人口的城市，你可以想象一个非常漂亮的城市只有20万人，那些大院子里头都是安安静静的，人也不多。

它当初是有一个规划的，中国建筑师协会的会长定的规划，就是所有的房子都是以保俶山为限度的，就是不能超过它，他定了这样一个规划，这个规划一直没有人敢破，就这个规划，第一个破这个规划的首先是望湖饭店，我们今天看望湖饭店也就是一个七八层高的，不算很高的房子，在当时已经是大家争论非常大了，而最后在杭州决定性的改变是新侨饭店，在杭州的第一个高楼，这就真的破了戒了，标志性的18层50米高的建筑。新侨饭店之后就是沿着延安路中国银行啊，这么一排房子过去，这样的话你从西湖边看过去就像是，这个尺度就变掉了，因为从西湖的苏堤看过去，城市应该是看不见的，这些房子一起来，整个就变了。这个事情发生都是八十年代末。事实上中国的很多城市包括杭州，都是曾经有过选择的可能，基本上都没有用这个办法，就是把老城保下来，在外面做一个新城。”

马修：
你2000年到这边以后，做建筑的体会多吗？除了教学，你还在做自己的事情吗？

王澍：
那时候建筑的活不多的，我主要是在做室内，但是我觉得是一个特别好的锻炼。学校当时办了一个装修公司，当时我们就做这些事情。接触了当时比如说城里，第一批富起来的人，因为装修会做餐馆的装修啊，那时候除了出租车司机，第一批挣钱的就是那些开小饭馆的人。而且都是文化水平不高的那么一批人，胆子比较大，先开始做。开个小服装店，开个小餐馆，开一辆出租车，还是那个状态。

因为那时候一些比较有意思的想法，就是那批人首先接受的。因为他们是为了竞争，所有人都在装修，我要做一个不一样的。越特别越好，因为我做的东西倒不算是很过分，但是非常的特别，记得当时甚至是接受了我那样的想法，我在湖山做过一个小的卡拉OK厅，他们说要变成一个小剧场，那我就起劲了，那时候是特别少的钱，当时一个卡拉OK厅只有两万多元人民币的装修，我后来想了一个主意，就是全部是用木头，大小一样的木条，我定了一个计划，我画了一个草图，完了我给工人看，我说从现在开始，我们连续24个小时，就按我的要求钉就行了，乱七八糟，像爆炸一样钉上去，全部钉满，说会不会掉下来，我说你们爬上去试试，几个工人上去像吊单杠一样。因为那些架子都咬在一起，所以它非常的坚固，整个就像一块木头被炸弹给炸开一样，那样一个空间就出来了。工人都不可想象，说装修还有这样干的。

马修：
这个城市发展越来越大，越来越快，对现在设计师或教育者会带来什么样的挑战、机会，或是责任？因为现在机会多了，你会怎样对你的学生讲如何对待这种状况？

王澍：
其实你看一下我的书里，谈得挺多的。我觉得不完全是文化的问题，很多人都会说这是什么东方西方文化冲突，我认为基本上也不是这样的事情。首先是现代建筑师你面对这种情况，需要对社会有一种伦理的责任。因为你想想有些东西，比如古建筑被拆除了，你觉得很遗憾，生活变得不安静你也会很遗憾，当然会遗憾。但有一点你不能忘了，我们碰到了一个非常特殊的时期，这个地球在100年前只有16亿人口，现在有将近67亿人口，这是历史上从来没有发生过的事儿，尤其是中国。

像我这两年做得比较多的一个工作，因为建设的速度很快，拆的房子很多，所以这两年我开始做这样一件事情，就是我的建筑比较多的使用别人拆掉的材料来建造，我用回收材料来造新房子。你如果明年再去看我们的象山校园的话，你会发现新造那一半，有很多房子是用回收材料造出来的。其它，在宁波我已经做了一些试验性的建造，整个学校都是我做的，前面做了一半，后面一半到明年夏天做完，前面一半就已经用了很多的回收材料，像里面用的瓦、砖、石头都是别人拆了之后我们拿过来的旧的，300多万件的旧材料，很多人看了很惊讶，因为没见过在中国一个新的大的设施，用那么大量的回收的旧的材料来做。

像我现在做的那个，我觉得实际上是一个反对浪费的做法。因为我觉得太浪费，这种做法。再一个，我对时间是特别的有感情，一个东西当它已经有了时间，我觉得它特别的美好，今天这种做法，看上去是在追赶时间，实际上是反对时间的一个做法，他把所有的一个旧的全都不要了，你新的东西是没有时间的。都是新的，我对这个一味的什么东西都要是新的是持怀疑态度的。因为生活一定是包含着，比如说你有回忆，是旧的，对吧？你不仅有愿望，有梦想，同时有你的回忆，这才是完整的。当你整个说都没有一个真正的回忆，回忆都变成是虚构的，比如说拍那种清朝的电视剧，虚构的回忆，都是变成虚构的时候，这个我觉得是满恐怖的一件事情。

我觉得这实际上是和这个社会的一些变化有直接关系。我觉得主要是这个原因，比如说建筑，建筑不是说，像中国，尤其是传统的建筑，一个设计师设计的一个社会上的项目的概念，比如说中国传统的住宅，它是有一个生活方式，一个文化的观念在里面，家族，氏族，佛家的礼仪，这些东西在里面，然后形成这样的一个形式，到今天的时候，你一看，整个社会结构已经变了。都是两个人带个小孩的这种小小的家庭，整个社会已经完全的分解掉了，这时候像那样的东西你不可能再继续下去，它是做不到的一件事情。当这种事情开始变化的时候，支撑建筑的最基础的东西不见的时候，你要硬想把它找回来，其实是非常困难，因为大家这个生活变掉了，不是这个生活了，所以这个时候可能是，我觉得是一个很有意思的时期，也是一个很重要的时期，就是你有没有可能重新塑造出一种真正比较有意义的生活方式，而且以建筑的方式进行表达。这不完全是靠建筑师可以做到的，你也可以设想说，我做成某种建筑会不会影响社会，你可以去想象，因为的确也会有这个，比如说像房地产商开发的这种住宅，你可以说它不好，但它是这时候的人的生活方式的最直接的一个表达，就是这样的房子，很小很小的单元，我们做这种房子的设计师非常困难的，因为它会每一户都不大，很小，完了每一户又要求是完全独立的，完了中国人又要要求这个房子要朝南朝北，还要通风还要采光，当这种要求下来的时候，这个事实非常难做的，但是你觉得会非常有意思，因为实际上是一个社会在重新整合它的生活形态和价值。

比如说在杭州还做过一个住宅，那也是一种试验，我也做高层住宅，100米高的这种高层住宅，就在钱塘江钱江三桥的这个桥头，我做的就是一个，所有的住宅都是一个两层的院子一样的东西摞起来的，我当时提出来，不管你住在多少米，你会认为你是住在两层楼里，你能看到房子有一个空间限定是两层的，你站在房子里你就知道这个房子是两层的。第二，我要让你在100米高，你也能种树。一般阳台可能1.5米，我的阳台可能就3米，非常深，它控制了这个阳台的空间，因此你感觉像一个房子，而不是一个阳台。

房子已经要开始发生变化，但是真正有意思的解决方式还没有完全出来，在这个时候我觉得，你可以觉得是一个很乱的时期，你也可以认为是一个很幸运的时期，因为你有机会在社会转型的时候，可能会做出某种东西，它会影响到超越很大一个时期的这种生活。

SUBURBAN FARMHOUSES 郊外农舍
ARCHITECTURAL ECLECTICISM
建筑折衷主义风格多样化过去与现在

在杭州市郊，先前占主导地位的大片农田，现在因为城市扩张而被挤得越来越小。从前在田里耕作的农民们慢慢把自己的土地拱手让给了开发商。此外，政府补贴和小规模副业使这些农民变得富裕起来。展现财富的一种方式就体现在他们的住宅上。这些农舍部分是民间建筑，部分像是迪斯尼乐园，本身就是直接模仿临近建筑的风格来设计构思的。有时两个邻居的住宅几乎一模一样。虽然差别很小，但对鼓励竞争及之后的设计发展而言意义十分重大。过去二十多年来，很多农民几次重建自己的房子，不仅是为了要跟上邻居们的步伐，而且要赶超他们。建筑设计师王澍把这个过程形容成是一种集体幻想。“如果每个人都设计出与别人完全不同的东西，那就是不正常的。每个家庭都给基本的设计增添一点不同的东西。为什么呢？因为需要比较和对比，否则就无法攀比。最后，人们被迫参与到这种集体的幻想当中去”。

尽管这些住宅通常只住一家人，但它们的富丽堂皇足以与城里的公寓相媲美，有五层之高，拥有多个房间、盥洗室和工作空间。这些五颜六色住宅的屋顶，有伊斯兰式的穹顶，有对艾菲尔铁塔的眷恋，也有的令人想起上海的东方明珠电视塔，它们高耸矗立直指天空。这种充满想象的、也许显得有些天真但具当地特色的建筑类型，是连贯的、特别的，而它的普遍性足以使其构成一个类别。

In the suburbs around Hangzhou, what was once predominately vast farmland is now being squeezed smaller by an expanding city. Farmers who previously worked the fields have slowly parceled out their land to developers. This coupled with government subsidies and small side businesses have made these farmers quite wealthy. One way of displaying this wealth is in their opulent homes. Part folk-architecture, part Disneyland, these homes are self-designed or conceived through directly imitating nearby designs. Sometimes it turns out that two adjacent homes are almost identical. While margins of difference may often be minuscule they are significant for encouraging competition and subsequent design developments. Over the last two decades many farmers have rebuilt their homes several times to, not only keep up with, but also, transcend 'the Joneses'. The architect Wang Shu described the process as a collective fantasy. "It would be abnormal if everyone designed something drastically different from others. Each household adds something different to the basic design. Why? There is a need to compare and contrast, otherwise, comparison would be untenable. In the end one is forced to participate in this collective fantasy."

While these residences usually house only one family, they are palatial compared to city apartments, boasting upwards of 5 stories, several rooms, bathrooms, and work spaces. Atop many of these colorful dwellings are Islamic-esque pavilions from which elaborate lighting rods, reminiscent of the Eiffel tower or Shanghai's Pearl TV tower, protrude upwards to the sky. This imaginative, perhaps naive and truly local, brand of architecture is consistent, peculiar and ubiquitous enough to constitute a phenomenon in itself.

BLUE GLASS 材质选择 —蓝玻璃

ARCHITECTURAL ECLECTICISM

建筑折衷主义风格多样化过去与现在

有一种关于中国建筑物上大量使用蓝色玻璃的说法，认为最初它是一种台湾或香港的进口产物[37]。的确，贝聿铭设计的声望极高的香港中国银行大厦就包裹在蓝玻璃形成的网格中，在1990年建成时，给大陆建筑设计师们带来极大的影响。杭州甚至有意要复制这座建筑。但是这种玻璃引入中国大陆其实更早，是在八十年代中期，蓝玻璃将天空强烈地反射出来，当时被认为象征了豪华。最初这种玻璃主要用于高档饭店和酒店，而一旦开始在本地生产，便被不加选择地运用，出现在各类建筑上，出现在城市和乡村。蓝色玻璃往往与白瓷砖一起使用，这造成了一种内外颠倒的浴室或被垂直竖起的游泳池的效果。而最近引进的环保色调的绿色玻璃常常配合米色瓷砖一起使用。尽管这种流行可能已经过了它的巅峰期，也很少用于新建筑，但在中国蓝玻璃仍然随处可见。

One theory about the abundance of blue glass used on Chinese buildings is that it was first introduced as a Taiwanese or Hong Kong import.[37] Certainly I.M.Pei's prestigious Bank of China Tower in Hong Kong, which is blanketed in a grid of blue glass, made a tremendous impression on mainland architects when it was built in 1990. Hangzhou even sports a replica of this building. But the glass arrived in China even earlier, in the mid-eighties, when its intensified reflection of the sky was considered a sign of luxury. At first it was mostly employed on fancy hotels and restaurants but once the glass began to be produced locally it was used indiscriminately, on every type of building, in both the city and countryside. Blue glass is frequently used in conjunction with white porcelain tiles, which has the effect of an inverted bathroom or vertical swimming pool. The recent introduction of the environmentally friendlier tone of green glass is often found in combination with beige tiles. Even though it probably has reached the peak of its popularity and is less frequently used in newer construction, blue glass is still found everywhere in China.

浙江省科协大楼
浙江皮塑大楼
辣妹子川菜
辣妹子川菜馆
杭州之江房

欢度国庆

APARTMENT COMPLEXING, NEW URBAN EDGES
公寓的小区化，新的城市边缘
ARCHITECTURAL ECLECTICISM
建筑折衷主义风格多样化过去与现在

过去十年间，将附近的村镇和小城市都包括在内，杭州整个城区扩大了三倍[38]。杭州近期获得的几处土地就位于钱塘江两岸。河流的一侧是钱塘新城，一排排新的高档住宅大厦向杭州一度无人问津的滨河边缘推进。另一侧则是滨江地带，坐落在杭州高科技产业开发区内，除了几家高科技工厂、写字楼和动漫工作室外，也已成为理想的新居住地。以豪华公寓大厦的形式出现的住宅，几乎一夜之间在各处耸立起来。就像上海的浦东一样，滨江也是短短几年之内在农田上建设起来的全新城区。按照业内人士王志刚的说法，外来有钱人因杭州的宁静而来此生活和投资，杭州的房地产市场被大大刺激起来[39]。这种投机性的房地产买卖或后来所谓“炒房”热（实际上将房地产作为股票来炒作）在杭州郊区一直很普遍，而钱塘江畔杭州一侧更为理想的住宅公寓则达到了相当高的业主占有率[40]。所有这些公寓都朝南面向钱塘江，这对中国消费者来说是极其重要的[41]，而且它们也在离杭州新政府区步行距离之内。钱江新CBD计划成为该市的新市区。这块占地10万平方米的区域包括了省市政府机构、地下购物中心、剧院、国际会议中心，计划入住达80万人[42]。

The city of Hangzhou has expanded threefold in the last 10 years enveloping nearby townships and smaller cities in its course.[38] Several of Hangzhou's recent acquisitions lie on either side of the Qiantang River. On one side of the river is the Qiantang New City that pushes out towards Hangzhou's once vacant waterfront edge with an army of new luxury residential high-rises. On the other side, known as Binjiang, lies the Hangzhou Hi-tech Industry Development Zone, which besides housing several hi-tech factories, office buildings and animation studios has also become a desirable new place to live. Residencies in the form of mammoth luxury apartment complexes have sprung up everywhere almost overnight. Like Pudong in Shanghai, Binjiang is an entirely new city district built over farmland in a matter of a few years.

According to Wang Zhigang, an industrial insider, wealthy outsiders buying into Hangzhou's tranquility for both living and investment stir up the real estate market in Hangzhou.[39] This speculative buying and selling of properties, or *chaofang* as it has come to be known (literally playing real estate property like stocks), has been common in Hangzhou's suburban districts while the more desirable apartments along the Hangzhou side of the Qiantang River have seen high rates of owner occupancy.[40] Not only are all these apartments facing south towards the river, something that is extremely important to the Chinese consumer[41], but they are also within walking distance of the new Hangzhou governmental district. The Qianjiang New CBD (Central Business District) is projected to be the city's new downtown area. This 100,000sqm area includes city and provincial government headquarters, underground shopping malls, a theatre, international conference hall and projected residences for 800,000 people.[42]

顺发恒业
佳境天城

中国100最佳楼盘
瑞立·中央花城
2万平米中央花园
四季花开，馨香满园
瑞立·中央花城
CENTER FLOWER CITY

阳
光
海
岸
Sunshine Coast
滨江·阳光海岸

光

APARTMENT COMPLEXING
REALIZING ESTATE: SUNSHINE COAST CASE STUDY
房地产业化——阳光海岸个案研究

Many of the newly built luxury complexes on Hangzhou's outer edges tower some 20 floors high and offer Western style amenities like lounges, gyms, and shopping centers. At the *Sunshine Coast* apartments, still under construction as of late 2008, two types of renovation styles are offered to the clients: "French Neo Classicism" and "Modern". Most customers chose the "French Neo Classicism", which offers a toned-down baroque milieu complete with lots of marble molding and chandeliers. According to Chen Xiaofeng, an agent for *Sunshine Coast*, classical western motifs evoke a sense of worldliness for these clients. "The apartment building is an imported Western concept", Chen argued, "It only makes sense to decorate these spaces in Western styles."[43]

In Spring, 2004 when the first apartments were built in the New City District they were sold for a modest 6-8000 RMB (US$880 -1180) per square meter. In early 2006, average housing prices in Hangzhou reached 10,000 yuan (US$1,470) per square meter.[44] In December 2008 The Binjiang Real Estate Group opened sales for *Sunshine Coast*, its fifth development project in the area. Within two weeks of being on the market over 70% of these pre-built units had been sold at an average cost of 2.3million USD each[45]; this is after the 2008 Global Credit Crisis. According to Chen most of the new owners are local Hangzhou-ers.

这些新建成的豪华公寓大厦高达20层，提供了西式的环境，诸如休闲设施、健身房和购物中心。到2008年底仍在施工中的"阳光海岸"公寓为客户提供了两种装修风格："法国新古典主义"和"现代派"。大部分顾客选择了法国新古典主义，运用大量的大理石和吊灯做装饰，带来一种柔和的巴洛克式环境。据阳光海岸代理人陈晓峰说，西方古典基调给客户带来一种很国际化的感觉。陈晓峰主张："公寓建筑是舶来的西方概念，只有按照西方风格来装修这些空间才会合理"[43]。

2006年初，杭州住房价格平均达到每平米一万元[44]。2004年春，当新城区建成第一座公寓住宅时，是以每平米六千至八千售出的。这个价格到2006年1月开始大幅度上涨。到2008年12月，滨江房产集团启动了阳光海岸的销售，这是该集团在这一地区的第五个开发项目。上市两周内，70%的住房以每套平均二百三十万美元的价格售出[45]，这就发生在2008年全球信贷危机之后。按照陈晓峰的说法，新业主大部分都是杭州本地人。

PART 3

THE PERFORMATIVE IN ARCHITECTURE
建筑中的行为

“行为建筑(Performative Architecture)”通常被认为是一种建筑类型，其中建筑的性能（其能耗、功能等等）是设计的主导原则。而建筑中的行为则涵括了同样的领域，当然也充斥着矛盾。

一幢建筑物与其居住者之间的关系究竟如何呢？居住者又如何处理那些基本上是强加于他们的建筑和工程施工的不当呢？“即兴而为”在答案中占了很大一部分。而行为就是由建筑的居住者、管理者或开发商不断对建筑物的外观进行的微妙处理。这也是一种有机的、动态的关系，随着时间的推移，在一开始就已经固定下来的背景当中添加和去掉一些成分。在杭州，气候是行为的最大因素。很多情况下，行为便是悬挂晾晒衣物、安装空调、电扇和饮水机。

尽管“行为建筑”意味着绿色环保意识，但这里引用的几个例证讽刺性地突出了中国的经济革命给大自然敲响的不祥丧钟。

'Performative Architecture' is commonly thought of as a type of architecture in which a building's performance (its energy consumption, functionality, etc.) is a guiding design principle. 'The Performative *in* Architecture' covers the same terrain, albeit postscript and paradox ridden.

What is the relationship of a building to its occupant? How does an inhabitant deal with the inadequacies of an architectural and engineering arrangement that has essentially been forced upon them? Improvisation is a big part of the answer. The Performative is the constantly changing, subtle manipulation of a building's architectural appearance by one's occupants, managers, or developers. It is an organic and dynamic relationship where items are added and removed over the course of time in a context that has been fixed from the start. In Hangzhou the climate is a large instigator of the Performative. In some instances it is the hanging of laundry or the installing of exterior mounted air conditioning units, fans and water machines.

While 'Performative Architecture' implies the notion of Green ideology, several of the examples cited here ironically underscore the unfortunate toll that China's economic revolution has taken on the environment.

HANGING AS ARCHITECTURE
外挂物——建筑的附属
THE PERFORMATIVE IN ARCHITECTURE
建筑中的行为

杭州是一个闷热潮湿的南方城市，年平均气温达华氏64度，年平均降雨量达到57.08英寸，平均相对湿度为70%。这种极度的湿气在夏季蒸发成水汽，所以洗净的衣物很难晾干。尽管大部分家庭现在都配备了洗衣机，但电动烘干机还不多见，而且价格昂贵。因而，衣物被褥便被一排排挂在所有能够利用的窗台、阳台、临时晾衣架甚至电线上干燥晾晒。这些附加设施处在随时不断变动的状态中。它们不但充斥着主体建筑，而其本身也成为临时的构筑物。这种居民同建筑及其周边环境的行为关系，成为这座城市的建筑、城市布局甚至文化的一个主要部分。今天，悬挂物在这座城市1980年代和1990年代间建成的公共住宅建筑中是最常见的。悬挂不仅不消耗能源，而且使建筑物保持阴凉隔热。不幸的是，随着物质财富允许越来越多的人用电器设备来烘干衣物，这种有利环境的做法逐渐在没落。

Hangzhou is a hot, humid, southern city with an average annual temperature of 64°F, an average rainfall of 57.08 inches and average relative humidity of 70%. This intense moisture, which literally steams in the summer, makes it difficult to dry one's laundered clothes. While most homes are now equipped with washing machines, electric dryers are still uncommon and expensive. Consequently garments and bedding are strung out to dry or air out on every available windowsill, balcony, improvised clothes rack and even on electric lines. These affixations and appendages are in a state of constant improvisational flux. They not only permeate the host architecture but also become momentary structures in themselves- a soft architecture of sorts. This performative relationship of the inhabitant to the building and its immediate surroundings has become an integral part of the city's architecture, urban topology and perhaps, culture. Today exterior clothes hanging is most commonly found on the city's public apartment buildings that were built during the 80's and 90's. Not only does hanging consume zero energy but it keeps the building shaded and insulated as well. Unfortunately this environmentally friendly practice is on the wane as material wealth is allowing more and more people to electrically dry their clothes.

中建七局上海
专修售
全站仪
经纬仪
水准仪
GPS测距仪 对讲机 望远镜
杭州光电仪器商行
杭州光电仪器商行
州国晟网吧
丰都茶业

浙A 4 0-5 8 3
A·40583
浙A·56491

生活
Life

250

FENG SHUI 风水
THE PERFORMATIVE IN ARCHITECTURE
建筑中的行为

在中国文化当中，柔和的风和清洁的水往往同好收成和良好的健康状况联系在一起，因此"好风水"就意味着好运。风水是流传了三千多年的传统，平衡一个人周围环境中的能量，以确保健康、财富和好运。根据道教的信仰，大地是有生命力的，充满了"气"或能量，这种堪舆手法通常被用来确定建筑方位、周围空间以及建筑内部陈设的布局。一座建筑物的走向、周围的花园、花园中的水域以及其它自然因素从根本上都是支配这种大地能量的完整体系的组成部分。今天，中国正体验着前所未有的富足，但具有讽刺意味的是，大部分环境已经恶化了。清洁的饮用水的缺乏仅仅是一个复杂困境的一部分而已。

"威尔逊中心中国环境论坛"的一份报告就指出，有近七亿中国人缺乏安全的可饮用水[46]。这种状况在杭州所属的经济蓬勃发展的长江三角洲地区尤为严重。不仅世界自然基金组织指出，太平洋绝大部分海洋污染来自长江三角洲的工业排放[47]，而且《中国日报》也将该地区的污染称之为"必须排除的一颗定时炸弹"[48]。随着水源被工业增长所污染，饮用水的销量激增，从1999年的339万吨增长到2007年的1836万吨。有预测表明，中国的饮用水销量到2010年将超过3000万吨[49]。今天，饮水机已成为每个家庭和公司企业的必备物品。

有趣的是，电风扇（风）和饮水机（水）常常在同一个商店里一起出售。这两种物品一起销售仅仅是一种偶然呢？抑或是将过去的哲学思想同当代生活联系起来的一种方式呢？它们是否是能量平衡的传统与花园池塘在现代的本土化再现？或者仅仅表明了这些能量已不再被正视呢？

Feng shui literally translated means wind-water. In Chinese culture gentle wind and clear water have always been associated with good harvest and good health, thus "good *feng shui*" came to mean good fortune. *Feng shui* is the 3000-year-old tradition of balancing the energy in one's environment to assure health, wealth and good fortune. Based on the Taoist conviction that the earth is alive and possesses *qi* or energy, this geomantic practice has commonly been used to position buildings, the spaces around them, and the contents within them. A building's direction, the surrounding garden, bodies of water in that garden, and other natural elements are essentially part of an integrated system that harnesses the earth's energy. Today as China is experiencing unprecedented wealth, much of its environment has ironically deteriorated as a consequence. The lack of clean drinking water (*shui*) forms just one part of a complicated dilemma.

According to a report from Wilson Center's China Environmental Forum, nearly 700 million Chinese lack access to safe water.[46] This condition is even worse in the thriving Yangtze River Delta to which Hangzhou belongs. Not only does the World Wildlife Federation contend that the majority of marine pollution in the Pacific Ocean is due to runoff from the Delta[47], but China Daily called pollution in the area "a time bomb that must be defused"[48]. With water supplies infected by industrial growth, sale of drinking water has increased sharply, from 3.39 million tons in 1999 to 18.36 million tons in 2007. Forecasts show that China's sale of drinking water will exceed 30 million tons in 2010.[49] Today water dispensers have become an integral part of most every home and business.

Interestingly, electric fans, which produce wind (*feng*), and water dispensers for water (*shui*), are often sold together at the same establishments. Is it merely a consequence that these two items are sold together or is it a way of connecting past philosophies to contemporary life? Are they modern, domesticated reincarnations of individual gardens and ponds that traditionally kept energies balanced, or merely an indication that those energies are askew?

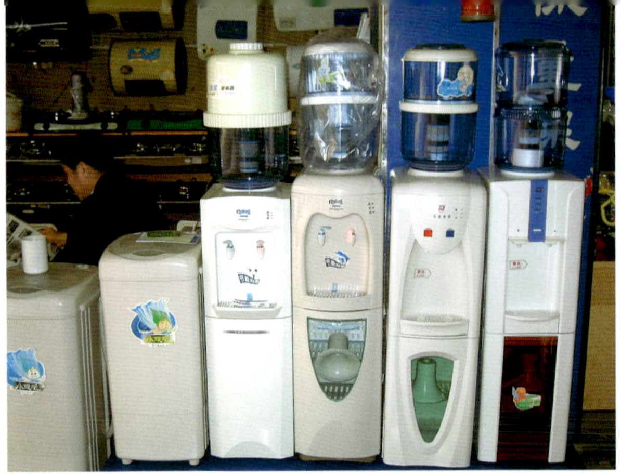

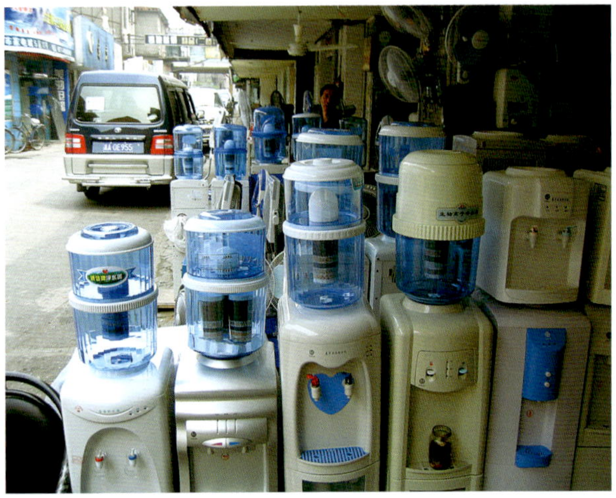

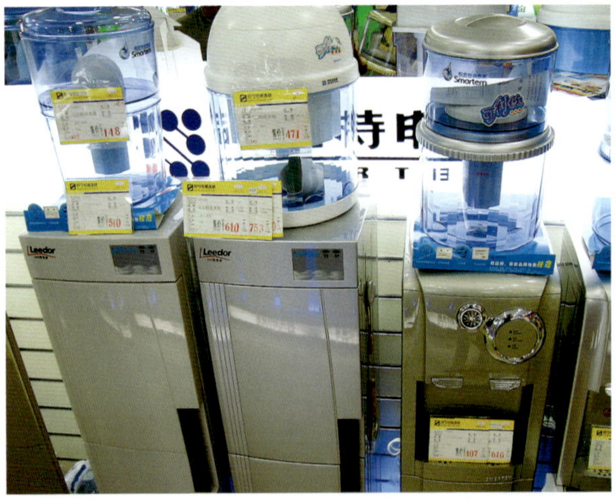

招工
茶
饮水机售价
台温机80元
台冰机198
立温机238
立冰电子298
立压机550
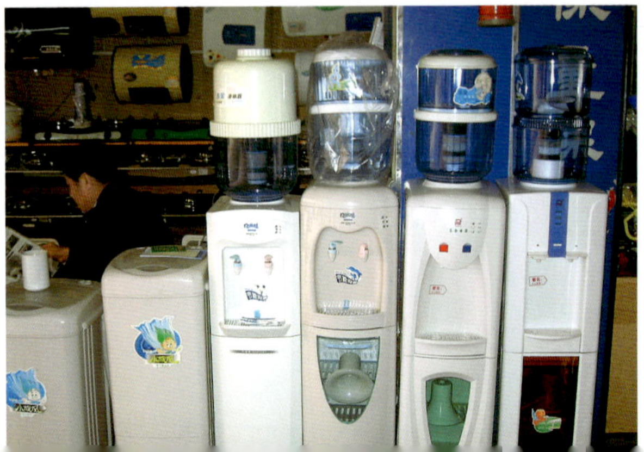

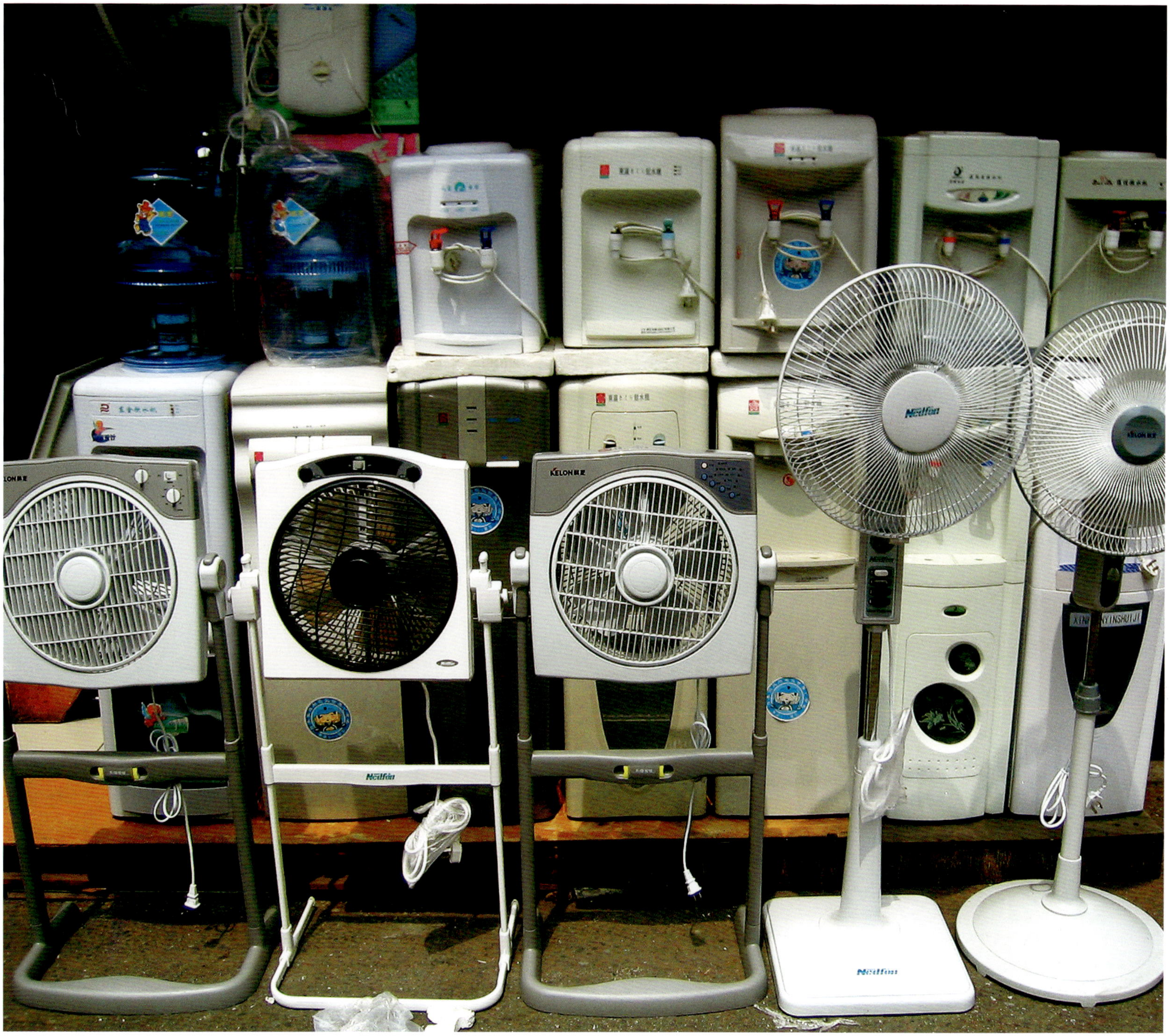
KELON
Nedfon

VERSACE
EYEWEAR

Luxury Water Dispenser
ESPL

AIR CONDITIONING AS EMBELLISHMENT
空调——作为一种修饰的调节
THE PERFORMATIVE IN ARCHITECTURE
建筑中的行为

和衣物被到处悬挂以及购买电风扇的理由一样，空调机在杭州的城市景观中也随处可见。闷热潮湿的气候使得空调，这个用来确保杭州日益增长的中产阶级凉爽舒适的工具显得十分必要。为了节约建设成本，施工建设项目很少安装中央空调系统，或者在建筑施工过程中仅被视为一种选择方案。用户负责安装和控制他们各自的空调系统。这就形成了在众多建筑物表面平添的一排排慢慢变化、杂乱不堪的空调主机。斑斑点点的建筑物表面往往破坏了一幢建筑物整体的统一性，成为杭州城市景观的一个有机组成部分。

空调这种“马赛克”也成为中国建筑耗能性低下的象征。《中国日报》援引建设部一份谴责开发商削减成本的报告说，2008年中国只有53%的新建筑符合国家节能标准[50]。效率低下、缺乏管理的空调系统无疑是无法符合这些标准的罪魁祸首。这些系统的精密性调节在世界其他地区已经司空见惯，却在中国被忽略了。目前政府还没有针对此类问题的规章制度，或者对此进行规范和控制的操控体系[51]。由于缺乏对这些设备的管理机构，日常生活中浪费了大量的能源，反过来又加剧了环境污染和自然资源的流失。

For many of the same reasons that clothes are hung everywhere and electric fans are purchased, air conditioning units also permeate Hangzhou's cityscape. The hot, humid weather necessitates the use of air conditioning to keep Hangzhou's growing middle class cool and comfortable. Due to economizing building costs, central air systems are rarely considered as an option during the building's construction. Instead each individual user is responsible for installing and controlling the use of their own units. This creates a slowly changing, anarchic array of AC appendages across the surface of many structures. The spotted facades, which often camouflage a building's architectural coherency, have become an integral part of Hangzhou's urban topography.

The air conditioner mosaic is also symbolic of poor energy performance in China's buildings. The China Daily, citing a Construction Ministry survey that blamed cost-cutting developers, said that only 53 percent of China's new buildings had met national energy conversation standards in 2008.[50] Inefficient and poorly managed air conditioning units have undoubtedly contributed to these failing standards. Unlike other parts of the world where fine-tuning of these systems is commonplace, it is often overlooked in China. There are no governmental regulations requiring it, or engineering bodies to regulate and control it.[51] The total lack of commissioning agents for these machines has routinely wasted serious quantities of energy, which in turn has contributed to environmental pollution and the draining of natural resources.

江城饭店

新丰小吃
金谷饭店
老百姓
大药房
博科
鼻炎水
19.6元
治鼻炎!

方正证券
FOUNDER SECURITIES

PART 4

THE SIGN AS A BUILDING
BUILDING AS SIGN
ADVERTISING'S CLAUSTROPHOBIA EFFECT
MICRO TO MACRO

作为建筑物的广告牌
作为广告牌的建筑物
广告的幽闭效应
从微观到宏观

中国的广告业是整个国家经济改革政策与实践的丰富多彩和迫切性的缩影。运用标语、广告牌、扩音喇叭以及大量其他媒介，宣告着中国已经进入了充满物质追求的全球化市场。开放市场就意味着开放营销，在两种情形之下公众都是不加质疑的目标，处于一个被动妥协的位置。商业广告信息从各个方向，以各种形式在公共场所发动着攻击。值得注意的，不仅是其一派热闹的景象，而是这种状况出现的速度。在三十年当中，中国从一个只有共产主义宣传标牌的国家，演变成一个被图像淹没的国度。今天，中国广告业的各项指数令人瞩目，2006年第一季度，收入达到1,555亿元人民币，比上年同期增长了18%[52]。自2005年12月10日中国广告市场对外开放以来，高额的跨国投资继续改变着这个行业的进程和量级。有人预测说，假定按照现在的发展速度，中国广告和媒体行业到2016年将成为全球第二[53]。

中国广告业迅猛发展，而这一发展恰恰同建设施工的环境有关，这也正是我的兴趣所在。在本章中，杭州各种不同的户外广告无处不在，将被作为一种城市现象来加以考察。虽然这些形式和方法当中，有些对于外界来说并不新颖，但是它为深入研究标牌的本质以及随着它对环境的普遍影响而令空间发生的改变，提供了一个机会。从微观的存在到宏观的表象，这一部分考察了杭州的标牌是如何构成的；这些广告设施和影像又如何影响着我们的个人空间、视觉感受、认知以及周围的建筑。

China's advertising industry epitomizes the colorful urgency of the nation's economic reform policies and practices. With banners, blurbs, loudspeakers and a multitude of other media, the announcement of China's arrival into the global marketplace is announced. Open market means open marketing, in both cases putting the public in the compromised position of unsuspecting target. From every direction and in every form a barrage of commercial messages makes its assault on the public domain. It is not so much the carnivalesque quality that makes this condition so remarkable but the pace at which these conditions arose. Within a period of three decades China went from a country where communist propaganda was the only form of public signage to an environment of inundating image spectacle. Today China's advertising industry figures are phenomenal. In the first quarter of 2006, its revenues stood at RMB155.5 billion (22.8 Billion USD), up by 18% compared to the same period a year before.[52] Furthermore since the opening of the Chinese advertising market to the outside world on Dec 10th 2005, tremendous multi-national investment continues to change the tenor and magnitude of the industry. Some have forecasted that given its current pace, the Chinese advertising and media industries will become the second largest in the world by 2016.[53]

It is the fury at which the advertising industry develops in China and how this development relates to the constructed environment that is of interest here. In this section Hangzhou's outdoor advertisements, in its many different and all pervasive configurations, are examined as urban phenomenon. Whilst some of these forms and methods aren't novel to the outside world it presents an opportunity to investigate the nature of signage and the commodification of space as it affects environments everywhere. From micro infestation to macro manifestations, this section inquires how Hangzhou's stratum of signs is composed; and how these advertising structures and images influence our personal space, visual perception, cognition, as well as the architectural surroundings itself.

MISCELLANEOUS SIGN FEST

混杂的牌子筵

SIGN AS BUILDING/BUILDING AS SIGN

作为建筑物的广告牌／作为广告牌的建筑物

杭州的广告牌是从底层开始起步的，比如凌乱的手写字条和自行分发的便条。用记号笔、喷漆或粉笔涂写的散工招牌上有这样的广告："配工具的电工"、"空调拆装维修"以及"管道疏通"。报摊和路边摊也宣传着电话卡存货，而旁边就是表明其合法性的营业执照。三轮车上悬挂的招牌写明了他们要回收哪些物品。电线杆上张贴着医治性病、赌博或寻人启示的复印广告。自行车和手表维修广告同降价销售及路边摊的菜单一争高下。

还有另一种临时的低保真广告。印有黄色或白色文字的红色横幅悬挂在树木、栅栏、窗户和围墙上，使整个杭州的街道成为一张错综复杂的网。这些红色横幅传播着当地政府的宣传口号，宣告着官方活动和公共服务信息。它们是这个无产阶级国家过去到处充斥的标语的残余，目前也被用于更商业的目的：庆祝建筑破土动工或者商店开张。

Hangzhou's stratification of signage begins at the base level, with a messy collage of hand-made and self-distributed notices. Scrawled in marker, spray paint or chalk, day laborer signs advertise "electricians with tools", "man with drill" and "unclog your sewer pipe". Newsstands and sidewalk vendors announce their inventory of calling cards next to registration placards that notify authorities of their legitimacy. Recyclers hang signs on their three wheeled carts specifying which materials they wish to collect. Xeroxes plastered on telephone poles advertise cures for sexually transmitted diseases, gambling tips, or plead for help in locating missing persons, while bicycle and watch repair signs compete with discount sale signs and the menus of makeshift kitchens.

Another stratum of temporary, lo-fi signage streams above the ground. Red fabric banners with simple yellow or white text are strung up on trees, fences, windows and walls forming an intricate web through the streets of Hangzhou. These red streamers spread local government propaganda, public service messages, and announce official events. Remnants of the nation's slogan-ridden proletariat past, as of late these banners have been employed for more commercial purposes: celebrating a building's construction or the opening of a store.

新身份证保护套
炒饭
炒年糕
炒粉干
水饺
美术培训
房屋出租
有三室一厅100多平方米的房屋出租，价格面议！
开水炉
13777823776
经营家具
办公桌、电脑桌、文件柜、
麻将桌、大衣柜、靠背椅、
方凳、沙发、床等。
有房出租
招聘
店面低价急转
画室出租
招工
学生食堂
厨师 面点师 各1名
电话：13148399958
寻人启示
宏春家电维修中心
修换拉链
修鞋
补衣服
修皮包
修拉链
修雨伞
麻辣烫 1.00
汤面 6.00元 牛肉面 6.00元
蛋炒饭 6.00元 砂锅粉丝 5.00元
炒年糕 6.00元 加量另算
米粉干
年糕
彩球坊迁至原大楼
(天风商厦)4楼422室
继续营业
电话：87030350 87010300
602
502
401
402
301
201

SIGN AS BUILDING
SUB-STRATA SIGNS
黄牛广告

SIGN AS BUILDING
RED BANNERS
红色标语

贺诺基亚杭州创新软件园顺利结顶
力拼搏奉献
尊重 热爱
以人为本
把脉经济 利国 利民
诚信待人 追求卓越
杭州营销中心
旅游集散中心武林广场
学习改变生活
贺欧神诺陶瓷杭州店盛大开业
预祝中国美术学院
中国美术学院2009届毕业生供需见面会

BUS SIGNS 巴士广告

SIGN AS BUILDING / BUILDING AS SIGN

作为建筑物的广告牌 / 作为广告牌的建筑物

单单有固定标牌还不够。杭州的公共交通体系也成为广告商们的主攻目标。乘坐公交车就如同置身于一片商业图像的海洋中。而候车亭的里里外外也都是定时更换的广告，以便保持广告的连续性。不仅空间被用来广告出租，时间也同样如此。按时间计算的广告出现在显示公交线路信息的设施上。安装在时间表和线路图上方的电视屏幕播放着商业广告、新闻和社会服务公告。公交车本身完全被一种乙烯广告所包裹，本质上已成为一个移动的、用于多种目的的标牌。行人和其他驾驶员可以从多个角度看到这个移动着的三维广告。这些意图明确的广告包装同时面向众多观众，不存在一般广告需要解决的广告的摆放与观众可视性的问题。在公交车内，用来支撑的横杆上也贴满了广告，而更多的则是移动电视里播放的充满软广告的节目。

Stationary signs are not enough. Hangzhou's public transportation systems have become prime targets for advertisers. The entire experience of taking the bus is infused with a myriad of commercial imagery. Bus shelters, both inside and out, bear advertisements that rotate periodically to reveal a continuum of ads. Not only is the space brokered for advertising purposes, but time is as well. Time-based advertisements also appear on structures that display bus route information. Mounted above the schedules and routes are video monitors that broadcast commercials, news and public service announcements. The bus itself is completely wrapped in a vinyl advertisement, in essence becoming a mobile, multipurpose billboard. Pedestrians and other drivers can view the moving, three-dimensional ad from many angles. These cleverly designed ad-wraps simultaneously address many audiences, doing away with the problem of sign positioning and audience access. Inside the bus, rungs used for bracing oneself are swathed with ads while more video monitors broadcast soft-advertisement infused programs.

松软好弹性！
活力有新招！
新
(汤大姐)

形象代言人：蒋雯丽

打响东方休闲之都品牌
创佳办公室
打响东方休闲之都品牌
争创中国最佳旅游城市
杭州市创佳办公室

五丰包点
松软好弹性！

OLYMPUS

绿
阿波罗男子
男科
To cure urology
体育场路58号
雪碧
透心凉
齐分享

黄色区域

THERMO KING
康师傅
茉莉清茶
花清香 茶新味

是关键
TIAN MU SHAN HOSPITAL
HANGZHOU · CHINA

商旅王
USB直插·短信王·双卡长待机
形象大使：刘德华

每晚20:30
经视新闻
王剑
李艳
王春

JOE ONE
九牧王服饰
MEN'S CLASSIC COLLECTION
中国驰名商标
横店影视城
浙江影视
PEPSI
百事可乐
招商银行 杭州分行
女儿红
中国驰名商标
卫浴
莱蒙商业中心：代言城市未来·成就商业典范
www.tefledu.org
黄龙精英中心
杭州市黄龙路5号
恒励大厦3楼B座
全国统一客服专线
Dream it,
Do it!
肯德基早餐

温州风味

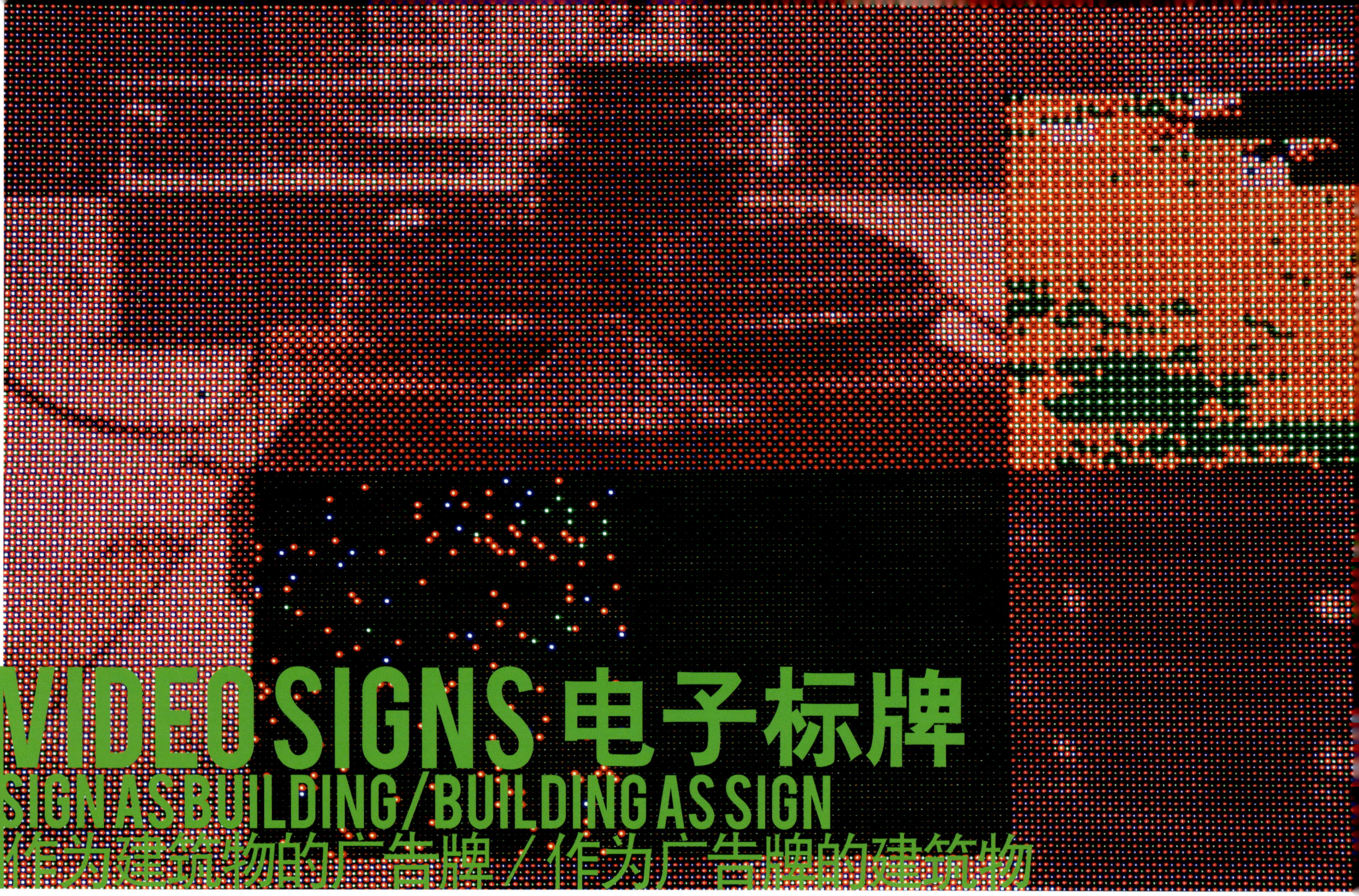

VIDEO SIGNS 电子标牌

SIGN AS BUILDING / BUILDING AS SIGN

作为建筑物的广告牌 / 作为广告牌的建筑物

按照世界生产电子标牌的先驱之一斯卡拉广播设备公司的说法，“视频标牌”就是那些用于展示广告的电视、电脑显示器和平板显示器之类的设备。就像世界上许多城市一样，杭州视频标牌的出现，是作为向目标消费者日益减退的注意力发起攻击及宣传的手段。这些广告牌播放着不断变化的声音和令人眼花缭乱的图像，而且也使得多个广告可以同时占据一个空间。从位于较私密的电梯和酒店大堂的小显示器，到店内多频道显示器，再到公共广场上的大型广告显示屏，这些以时间来计算的广告可以用多种形状和多种尺寸来播放（通常15至30秒钟——就象电视广告业一样）。

另一种动态电子标牌，采用的是液晶显示，循环滚动播出文字和图像。在杭州，这些信息丰富的广告牌通常在银行入口可以看到，用以播放产品和汇率。

According to SCALA Broadcasting, one of the pioneers of electronic sign manufacturing in the world, “video signs” are devices such as televisions, computer monitors, and flat panel displays that are used to display signage. Like many cities across the world the video sign in Hangzhou is emerging as a way to combat the diminishing attention span of targeted consumers. These signs not only dazzle with a constantly changing barrage of imagery and sound but also allow several ads to occupy a single space. From small monitors found in the more intimate spaces of elevators and hotel lobbies to multiple-channel, in-store displays to mega signs in public squares, these time-based ads (usually 15 to 30 seconds long - like television commercials) can be found playing in many shapes and sizes.

Another type of dynamic, electronic signage in the form of LED displays, rotate an endless, linear stream of text and image. In Hangzhou these information rich signs, usually employing red text, are commonly found at the entrance of banks advertising products and rates.

durex
SAMSUNG
SONY
SONY

L'OREAL

L'OREAL

L'OREAL

杭州剧院
凤凰都市传媒
省钱的卡、放心的卡
安心卡
共建新天水　共享新繁华
MINI CLUBMAN

中国建设银行
China Construction Bank
中信银行欢迎您光临!
中国建设银行
China Construction Bank
ICBC

ZARA
Häagen-Dazs
Häagen-Dazs
Häagen-Dazs
Häagen-Dazs
ZARA

SELF-STANDING STRUCTURES
独立构筑物
SIGN AS BUILDING / BUILDING AS SIGN
作为建筑物的广告牌 / 作为广告牌的建筑物

这种类型包括在杭州市内到处林立的大量独立广告设施。横在过街天桥侧翼的广告，从小企业招牌到麦当劳的M型，独立的招牌无处不在。不论这些招牌是装在框子里的菜单，还是加固的广告牌，都独立地耸立于建筑群当中，隐居闹市，并占据着它们各自的位置。这些大型招牌当中，有些体积十分庞大，结构设计也非常结实，有些则由四面墙组成，另外一些则牢固地贴在立柱上，甚至本身可以被视为一种建筑形式。

更大型的广告牌则通常立在偏远的高速公路旁或是拥挤的市中心高架路旁，面向杭州日益增长的流动人口。有统计数字表明，从2006年至2008年，杭州汽车总量实际上已增长到438,000辆[54]。全国的统计数字甚至更为令人惊讶——预计到2010年，中国公路上行驶的车辆将达到5,500万辆[55]。汽车数量激增使得城市规划者难以控制和调节基础设施、车辆登记注册以及路边广告牌的管理。当中国的汽车文化以破纪录的速度增长时，带来了拥堵、污染和路边广告牌的激增。宁波、杭州和上海之间延伸的280公里长的公路旁，排满了密集的广告牌，成交叉双行排列，充斥道路两侧。农舍栖身于这些广告牌组成的丛林之中，其中一些本身已成为广告牌。这些房子朝向公路的一面也都涂上了广告，大部分是用原色。最近，印刷乙烯广告开始取代这些手工绘制的广告，努力跟上更新的、更高水平的竞争。

This category encompasses the plethora of freestanding sign structures that are planted throughout Hangzhou. From small business signs to McDonald's arches to the mammoth triangular billboards that flank overpasses, freestanding signs are everywhere. Whether these signs are a menu mounted upon an easel or a reinforced signpost, they stand independently of any architectural apparatus, occupying their own ground as one structure among many in the congested urban center. Some of these larger signs, with their monumentality and robust engineering; some complete with four walls; others that pivot firmly on one column, might even qualify as a mode of architecture themselves.

Larger billboards, which are usually positioned along outlying highways or elevated roads downtown, address Hangzhou's growing mobile population. Statistics show that from 2006 to 2008 the amount of vehicles in Hangzhou practically doubled to 438,000.[54] The statistics for the entire nation are even more staggering - it is predicted that 55 million vehicles will be running on China's roads by 2010.[55] This rapid increase in the amount of automobiles makes it difficult for city planners to regulate infrastructure, registrations, and emissions, much less signage. As China's car culture grows at a record-breaking speed it brings with it congestion, pollution, and the proliferation of roadside billboards. Along the 280km of highway that stretches between Ningbo, Hangzhou and Shanghai lays a dense field of billboards that stand in a staggered double line formation and blankets both sides of the road. Amongst this forest of signs are farmhouses, some of which have also been converted into signs. The road-facing sides of these houses have advertisements painted on them, mostly in a palette of primary colors. Recently printed vinyl has begun to replace these hand painted signs in an effort to keep up with newer and taller competition.

COTTO 高陶
for Today's Lifestyle
原装進口衛浴
美加华
諾貝爾磁
品质生活值
专卖店
CRW
英皇卫浴
CRW SHOWER EQUIPMENT
顶尖卫浴专家 中国知名品牌
hzbank
杭州市商业银行
Hangzhou City Commercial Bank
XIANDAI
現代瓷砖
现代·生活 Modern life

English First
英孚教育
学英语，来EF!
English Changes Your Life!
www.englishtown.com

明湖苑
欢迎光临

新中源
新中源陶瓷
NEW ZHONG YUAN CERAMICS
打造建陶国际品牌
中国驰名商标
中国名牌
国家免检产品
杭州君临建材有限公司总代理
中国著名品牌
BOHUA 博華陶瓷
网址: www.bohua2000.com
MOEN® 摩恩
杭州陶瓷品市场8厅78号 电话: 86088888
东鹏陶瓷
特惠一口价!
东鹏 珊瑚玉
聯興古典磚
ISO9001:2000 国际质量体系认证
杭州联合银行
United Rural Cooperative Bank of Hangzhou
让
TOT

诚 聘
服务员 若干名
迎 宾 1名
收银员 1名
切 配 2名
洗碗工 2名
江干名车长廊
轩逸
优雅同行
sanxin
三新厨房精品馆
即将开业
McDonald's

中德汽修

财智国际惟有地段不可复制
vip:(86).575 84111666
省级开发区
滨海工业区
请系好
安全带

国家级
诚邀加盟
上海机电城
021-6250 9900
婷微科技
100

JKJ
杰凯拉链

竞价发布 报名截止日：
www.hzjcgg.com
媒体供应商：杭州萧山国际机场高速广

塘新线新农桥、九
号坝桥封闭施工。
一切车辆请绕行

SIGN AS BUILDING
HIGHWAY: BILLBOARDS
高速公路：广告牌

SIGN AS BUILDING
HIGHWAY: FARMHOUSEBOARDS
高速公路：农舍侧墙的标语

申水管道
SHENSHUI PE PPR PVC
销售服务: 400-888-1117
达欧焊机
品质见证实力
0576-86491115
0572-3670006
抗干扰磁芯
0576-84 010918
3150吨锻造水压机
太和锻造 浙江台州
为您提供0-35吨锻件
常胜将军
鼎浩吹塑机
Blow Molding Machine
0576-84022888
益泉·世纪
宏远数控机床
0572-3670006
三江超声波
焊接机 清洗机
TINCOO
鼎浩吹塑机
Blow Molding Machine
0576-84022888
www.Tincoo.com
飞天广告:13706766592
0574-880 55298
三江超声波
清洗机 焊接机
厂址:宁波联丰中路望春工业区
鼎浩吹塑机
Blow Molding Machine
0576-84022888
0576-84 010918
3150吨锻造水压机
太和锻造 浙江台

CROWNING 屋顶皇冠

SIGN AS BUILDING / BUILDING AS SIGN

作为建筑物的广告牌作为广告牌的建筑物

“屋顶皇冠”其实是位于建筑物顶部放置广告牌的附属设置，它们无处不在。这些沉重的金属构架使建筑物向上延伸（有时高达七米），因此加高了建筑物而破坏了建筑原有的美感。夜晚整个广告被点亮，这些突出物就像是一顶皇冠的尖角。这种情况下，广告占据了另一个新的领域——建筑物上方的领空，从远处一眼便可以望见，这种“皇冠”面向的是杭州那些穿行于城市诸多高架路的最高处的移动消费者。按市规划委的说法，西湖区2003年后任何建筑物上搭建这种屋顶构筑物都是非法的。这是市政府首次颁布有关该市户外广告的规章制度[56]。

Crownings are the ubiquitous structural additions placed on the roofs of buildings that carry advertisement billboards. These heavy metal frames essentially extend the building upwards (sometimes to seven meters or more) and alter the original architectural aesthetic by literally capping it. Sometimes these structures have poles that feather out like the points of a crown and light the advertisement at night. Advertising in this case occupies another new territory - the air space of a building, and while visible from far and wide, the crown also addresses Hangzhou's mobile consumers traveling atop the city's many elevated highways. According to the Urban Planning Committee, crowns were outlawed on any buildings built after 2003 in the West Lake district of Hangzhou. It is the first attempt of the city government to impose any regulations on outdoor advertising in the city. [56]

日立空调 洗衣机
美的中央空调
杭州就业训练中心
ups
Meters/bonwe
lesles
MARY KAY
上海浦東發展銀行
中国银联
SUPER 8 MOTEL
可口可乐
人间天堂新湖
东方金座
专享西湖的酒店式私家
售楼热线 0571-8707115
杭州市外经贸局
真功夫
健康你我他
欢乐千万家
杭州娃哈哈集团公司
汽车价值的典范
乡村树

之江水泥
坚塔商砼
JTST
构筑天堂硅谷
浙江省之江水泥有限公司 86616178
杭州坚塔混凝土有限公司 86631888 86631999

嵋山·金马地板
香港金马国际集团有限公司 8698 5521

Coca-Cola
广告位招商 87806989

四季鞋都 · 源头之都
四季鞋都
更多选择 更多惊喜
闪亮登场
四季鞋都
盛世钱塘

中国电信
CHINA TELECOM
世界触手可及
我的e家
爱没有距离 家就在身边
精彩信息
用心服务

唯一指定用车：北京现代

全球通 GoTone
专家品质 信赖全球通
全球通 GoTone
底价极限
移动营业中心
浙江大学医

中国建设银行 建设
CCB Builds M
中国建设银行

无所

远东电缆
GUERLAIN

Fiat Siena

VIOLET SALOON
意大利·紫依沙龙 商务休闲装
杭州大厦B座8楼 纤体热线:8510 8200
www.mariefrance.com.cn
武林路
WULIN ROAD
西湖风景区
WEST LAKE SCENIC AREA
庆春路
QINGCHUN ROAD
浣纱路
HUANSHA ROAD
湖滨路
HUBIN ROAD
延安路
YANAN ROAD
长生路
CHANGSHENG ROAD
客
停

中国建设银行
China Construction Bank
客户服务热线：95533
网址：www.ccb.com
建行电子银行

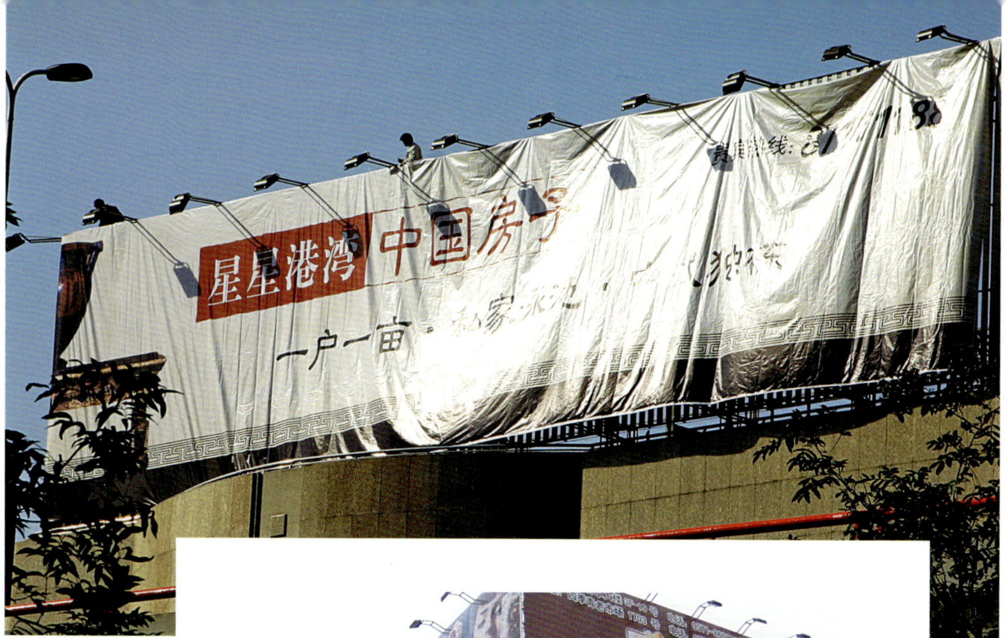
星星港湾
中国房子
一户一亩

Na

莎梓迪卡 国际服饰
浙江总代理
JIEAO 杰奥

Marco Polo
馬可波羅
马可波罗瓷砖
MARCOPOLO TILES
杭州长红公司总代理
TEL: 86085753 86086309

前
進

中洲大厦
ZHONG ZHOU MANSIONS
中洲娱乐城
中洲童装区
友龙酒家

PLACARDATION 张贴

SIGN AS BUILDING / BUILDING AS SIGN

作为建筑物的广告牌/作为广告牌的建筑物

张贴广告是依据可用性和可能性，将广告随机张贴在建筑物或设施的不同部位的做法。这种做法通常导致了随意插空张贴，遮挡了建筑物的表面。建筑物带着这些仿佛其本身附属品一样的广告，正如19世纪西方城市张贴的小广告和广告牌。广告被相继贴在建筑物上，通常并不事先考虑意图。这是一种即兴的张贴，让人想起棋盘游戏，但却是在建筑物的表面。张贴通常是根据建筑物所有者的一时兴起以及广告的逻辑。广告招贴被贴在最容易被看到的地方，通常最靠近街道，好让路人看见，或贴在高处让远处的人看到。尽管杭州市对于张贴任何类型的广告都有严格的登记程序，但据市政管理部门说，对于建筑物上广告的尺寸和张贴并没有具体限制，只要不超出建筑物本身的大小即可[57]。这些张贴广告不仅可以在建筑物上看到，而且在城市的许多桥梁、地面和地下通道上都可以看得到。

Placardation is the system of randomly attaching signs to different areas of a building or structure based on availability or opportunity. The process usually results in a haphazard patchwork that masks what would have been the building's facade. The building wears the sign as an accessory much like the placards that were worn by street vendors and human billboards during the nineteenth century in Western cities. Signs are placed onto the building sequentially, usually without any prior consideration of a master design. It is an improvisational arrangement reminiscent of a board game - played out on the surface of a building. Placement is usually based on the whims of the building's owner and the logic of advertising. Signs are placed where they are most visible, usually closer to the street for the passer by and high atop the building for those far away. While there is a rigorous registration procedure for mounting any type of sign in Hangzhou, according to The Office for Urban Management there are no restrictions regarding size or placement of signs on buildings, as long as it doesn't exceed the building's own dimensions.[57] These placards are not only found on buildings but also on the city's many bridges, under and overpasses.

东方中汇
杭州
2006
健身中心
87048808
皇家桌球会
杭州市台球协会
台球培训中心
Tel: 87217786
晨光健身中心
CHENGUANG JIANSHEN
足浴 棋牌
Tel:87234887
杭州市建设工程规划告示牌

九鼎装饰
国盛装饰
君威國旅
KingWay Travel
好伦哥
日式拉面

唐鹰
裤子与生活的艺术
TON EAGLE
唐鹰西裤
中大装饰
香山瘦身
瑞得

九星服
貿服飾
中国联通
CHINA UNICOM
超越梦想
引领未来
联通新时空CDMA——新一代移动通信
华硕W6 轻薄美型 醉出色
华硕W6笔记本电脑
臺灣精緻農特產展
新世纪装饰材料市场
浪漫一身
服饰展示中心
裤业批发
男女时装
杭州 电力
四季服装城
浙江九星
乔山国际健康科技集团
JOHNSON HEALTH TECH CO.,LTD.
文体市场
Canon
佳能计算器
忆和电子
专业销售
SOEASIES
数易通
万年青健身器材杭州总汇
三新集团
THREE GROUP
东方灯饰市场
北欧风情
向前 900 米
新科隆地板

曲美婷
QuMeiTing
一次成型 无缝美体
开开牌内衣 中国驰名商标 总代理：环北市场二楼一区 17–18 号 加盟热线：0571–87216564 13905714813（徐）
富妮来
funilai
富妮来
2005/06
FUNILAI COLLECTION
·家居休闲服·
加盟热线 0760－2120959
轻轻松松富妮来
美国花雨伞集团（香港）有限
温馨提示
爱国守法
明礼诚信
团结友善
勤俭自强
货运
环北运输公司
航铁汽
空路运
全国各地

四方
87225644
手机: 13805712208
Natural life
感觉与众不同
Modal
LYCRA
meisee
美思
广东省著名商标
中国内衣行业"十大品牌"
STI
诗婷
环北情意浓 市场为大众
隐患险于明火 防范胜于救灾
OYI 欧耶
0571-87219571
13805728023
富妮来
广东省著名商标
健将
爱莎
杉杉内衣系列
CLASSIC GARMENTS FASHION TRENDS
国际品牌形象
迪诺兰顿服饰
落实长效管理机制
人民生命至上
增强防火意识 场内严禁吸烟
营造市场安全环境
防火重于泰山
环北是我家
严禁计划外生育
新杭派休闲服饰城
米歌服饰(香港)有限公司
常青意法

2006
杭州世界休闲博览会
TAXI

Kingston 金士顿 — 全球存储领袖
www.kingston.com/china
佳能产品专卖

国家免检
国家3C产品认证
杭州绿保建材有限公司总经销 联系电话:0571-86082039
鹰牌卫浴
EAGLE BRAND SANITARY-WARE
品质好 生活好
健康看得见!
地址:杭州绿保建材有限公司总经销 展厅电话:0571-86081291 售后服务电话:0571-86082039
MICAWA美加华
中国卫浴专家
法恩莎卫浴
FRENZA
进口意大利

中国平安 平安中国
便捷省心
通话天下
17909
主叫IP电话
江城饭店
杭州四季青服装市场
欢迎您
LAVIDA 朗逸
新月·东方
CRESCENT EAST
浙江省汽车市场
配件用品 新旧车交易
华浙鞋包商城
OFFICE HELP
办公助手
配送办公用品的专业企业
电动车超市
打造"平安上城"
创建和谐湖滨
佳丽摄影
KANGWEI
1F 陶瓷卫浴
2-3F 宾馆酒店用品
4F 地板超市
新一代天籁
NISSAN旗舰 舒适尊享
文体市场
WEN TI SHI CHANG
金康普力
杭州体育文化用品市场
CAMRY

DEVISED VEILING 设计的面纱

SIGN AS BUILDING/BUILDING AS SIGN
作为建筑物的广告牌/作为广告牌的建筑物

尽管一些建筑物上的广告牌是随意的，但也有些是预先构思出来的，并且按照有条不紊的体系展示出来。但是在另外一些情况下，建筑物上的广告牌却是在不断增添和削减的过程中产生的，这些建筑物上的广告在建筑施工前，即建筑设计阶段就已经存在了。广告牌以及悬挂广告的附属设施都是专门为建筑物外墙设计的。就像窗户和拱腹（有时在这些建筑物中被废弃了，以便加大广告空间），广告由于具有必要性和实用性而被统一纳入设计蓝图中。

这种建筑样式可以与文艺复兴时期的浅浮雕相比较，将宗教叙事纳入建筑物的整体设计中[58]。在杭州，市场营销已有意在设计过程中被优先被考虑了，往往带来了对广告空间功能化、结构化以及最大化的利用。很多时候，在整个建筑物表面，相互竞争的广告牌之间的空隙成了唯一可以看得到建筑物本身的地方。

While some signs on buildings are applied haphazardly others are preconceived and laid out in an ordered system. Whereas in other examples, signage on buildings results from an ongoing process of adding and subtracting, the billboards on these buildings existed prior to construction, in the conception stage of the building. Spaces for billboards and apparatus' to hang them are specifically designed onto the building's exterior wall. Like windows and soffits (sometimes forgone in these buildings to maximize ad space), signs have been integrated into the blueprint as a necessary practicality.

This mode of architecture could be compared to Renaissance era bas-reliefs, which integrated religious narratives into the building's overall design[58]. In Hangzhou the iconography of marketing has been conscientiously prioritized into the design process, often resulting in a functional and structured use of ad space. In some instances the entire facade, save the divisions between competing signs, is completely covered in signage.

CASCADE
展厅地址：杭州陶瓷品市场4厅2楼8号
服务热线：0571-86085740
TEL：0571-86081400
欧宝建材
升华陶瓷
SHENGHUA CERAMIC
国家免检产品
超越一个石代
3T 技术
RGC
仿古砖专家
荣高陶瓷
国家免检产品·中国陶瓷行业名牌产品·广东省名牌产品
QHTC
强辉
精工砖
法恩莎卫浴
FRENZA
ARROW
箭牌卫浴

打造建陶国际品牌
新中源陶瓷
NEW ZHONG YUAN CERAMICS
American Standard 美标
ARROW
箭牌卫浴
国家免检
中国名牌
3C认证

羅馬
中国著名品牌
OHUA 博
楠宋酒店设备用品

意法服饰 批发市场
CQ&IF
杭州常青意法服饰城
PEOKER
bellbird
风铃鸟
TOOLSTON
天明

意法服饰
RubyDives
Wealthy
bellbird
风铃鸟
Maneas
羽绒服

清华阳光
大管换代—太阳能进入紫金TT时代
本市场一楼57号 电话:86984881 服务热线:88940757
领跑世界·格力空调
GREE 格力
西子德贝
先锋电器
樱花
照材婚纱城

陶坊
JODEN
乔登卫浴
KOHLER
科勒厨卫经典
马可波罗磁砖
MARCOPOLO TILES
ARROW
箭牌卫浴·瓷砖

乐购 Hymall
欢乐购物每一天
乐购 Hymall
欢乐购物每一天

金成窗帘
毛皮布行
好呢绒 瑞福生
金星布艺
电话：86947611 86990402 86994856
软体床 窗帘

21金维他
家人的健康
我们的责任
乐购
快乐家居 温馨生活
TEXTILE ZONE

PLAZA
美食天堂
工联精品服饰城

E·SHOW 锦衣馆
韩国指甲油

morgan
MORGAN

地址：杭州市延安路龙翔大厦7216号
加盟热线：0571-87781303
龙翔服饰城

BOSIDENG
界品牌 民族骄傲
拒水 拒油 拒污
国销量遥遥领先
SPRING SUMMER

高级男士商务休闲系列
Entica
安迪卡
/国际经典品牌/
文倩服饰
龙翔服饰城

雅戈尔
服饰专卖
地址：电力服装城2F-2140
电话：0571-86982015
BARBARA
类 批 发 区

PROJECTURE, THE DECORATED DUCK
突出物，盛装的鸭子
SIGN AS BUILDING / BUILDING AS SIGN
作为建筑物的广告牌/作为广告牌的建筑物

建筑物成为广告牌，而广告牌又成为建筑物。在城市购物中心及其仓储区，整个设施或建筑表面都挂满了广告。从地面到屋顶，在那些原本是窗户的地方，悬挂着巨幅广告标语。在中国，便宜的喷绘印刷使得小公司都负担得起大幅广告。随着户外乙烯彩色印刷成本降低到每平方米只有10元人民币，整个建筑物有时对于野心勃勃的广告商们来说还不够大。这些建筑物实际上充当了这些乙烯横幅的悬挂设施。而建筑的功能完全服从于市场竞争的冲动。

《向拉斯维加斯学习》的作者将这种建筑体系称为“经过装饰的大棚”，实际上是一个直接遵从其规则的空间和结构有机体。事实上，这部分引用的众多例证，都可以被视为“经过装饰的大棚”，广告招贴成为建筑格局的组成部分，有助于推进市场营销活动。在《向拉斯维加斯学习》当中，作者进而将“经过装饰的大棚”同另一种被称为“鸭子”的建筑体系相比较。“鸭子”的得名是来自一座外观看起来很像鸭子的建筑物（长岛鸭场），而且暗指一种沉浸在整体象征形式之下的建筑体系。在“突出物”部分所展示的例证当中，出现了这两种体系之间的融合，建筑物的符号化外观成为一个三维的广告牌。不论这是一个经过装饰的鸭子，还是一个已经完全淹没在各种装饰之下的大棚，尚有待争论。在这种情形之下，广告牌就是一座建筑物，而建筑物也就成为了广告牌。

A building that is a sign and a sign that is a building. Both in the city's shopping center as well as in its warehouse district, entire structures or surfaces of many buildings are articulated by and of signage. From the ground to the roof, over what would be windows, hang advertisement banners. In China, inexpensive, large-format printing has made bigger advertising more affordable for smaller companies. With outdoor vinyl printing costs as low as ten yuan (1.33 USD) per square meter, entire buildings sometimes are not large enough for ambitious advertisers. These buildings literally act as a structure from which the vinyl banners project. Here the functionality of architecture is one that is totally submitted to the impulse of market competition.

The authors of *Learning from Las Vegas* identify this architectural system as "the decorated shed", an organization of space and structure that is directly at the service of its program. In fact many of the examples cited in this section can be considered "decorated sheds", where signs have become part of an architectural configuration that helps drive market activity. In *Learning from Las Vegas* the authors go on to contrast the "decorated shed" with another architectural system that they call "the duck". "The duck" takes its name from a building that is actually shaped like a duck (The Long Island Duckling), and indicates an architectural system that is submerged by an overall symbolic form. In the examples shown in *Projecture* a fusion of these two systems occur whereby the symbolic form of the building is a three-dimensional billboard or a sign. Whether this is a "decorated duck" or a shed that has been submerged entirely under decor is left to argue. Either way in this case, the signs are a building and the buildings are signs.

大庄
大庄
地板大卖
soilm
索姆橱
Internationalization Cupboard
世界领先的橱柜品牌
佳好佳
EleganT
质量担保 先行赔付
瓷砖卫

佳好佳
居饰商城
大庄
地板大卖场
soilm 索姆橱柜
佳好佳
瓷砖卫浴
大卖场

打造杭城品牌居饰商城
比品牌.比价格.买的就是
ARROW
箭牌卫浴
九鼎装饰
0571-86990000
CASCADE
卡思卡特
CLIPSAL 奇胜
staron 星容
SAMSUNG
华通水电

新海油漆超市
中豪装饰材料市场
二楼地板区
8店同庆
"总督漆"进驻浙江市场8周年
多买多送!
生牌漆
浙江名牌
经典漆
经典防氧墙面
立邦全效合一
NIPPON PAINT
ALL IN ONE

国家双免检产品
藍鳥壁紙
偉龍牆紙
WILAND WALLCOVERINGS
TCL国际电工

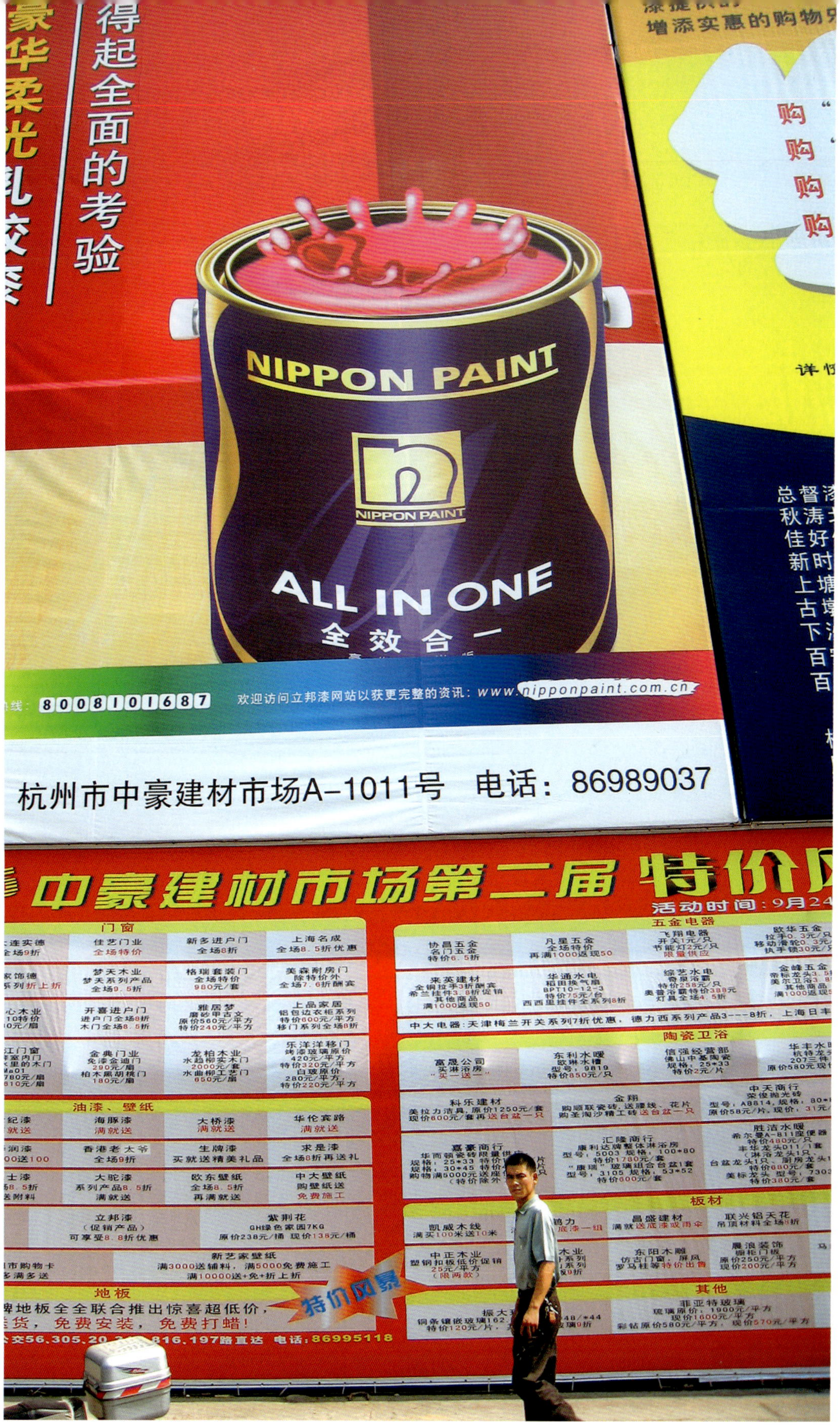
得起全面的考验
NIPPON PAINT
ALL IN ONE
全效合一
8008101687
欢迎访问立邦漆网站以获更完整的资讯: www.nipponpaint.com.cn
杭州市中豪建材市场A-1011号 电话: 86989037
中豪建材市场第二届特价风
门窗
五金电器
陶瓷卫浴
油漆、壁纸
板材
地板
其他
特价风暴

明成地板
星月
德威
华丰五金
新科隆地板

EUROART
欧雅壁纸
ARROW

新世纪
杭州墙纸批零中心
dada
哒哒厨柜
4180元/套
只有低价拒绝劣质
国家双免检产品
偉龍牆紙

中建名贵地板
万森地板
WANSEN FLOOR
华鑫装饰材
Der
PACO

OPEN
Konica柯尼卡
新世纪
CENTURIA SUPER

帝王洁具
monarch sanitary ware
Der 德尔地板
0571 8699 1535
800 828 2939
www.der.com.cn
华威楼梯扶手
佳华梯业商行
万能角钢货架

三新集团
THREE GROUP
东方灯饰市场
灯饰市场
华东家电市
60

东方家私
吉盛伟邦家居广场
四、五楼
杭州东方家私市场
双叶家具
SHUANGYE

宝塔漆
圣丹漆
2F 门 窗 城
1F 油漆、墙纸
华通水电
世友地板

双叶家具
SHUANGYE
床垫

杭州东方家私市场

东方灯饰市场
T&J 天基
The Noble Choice
ELECTRIC
英国专业 天基电气
deco
杭州售后服务热线：0571-87041525
CLIPL
东方灯饰市场
秋涛北路137号

东方家私
香港十大品牌
中豪建材装饰市场
地址：秋涛北路80号 电话：0571-86992324

邀加盟:86435877
品质保证
圣丹
料市场十大优秀品牌
圣丹漆
3C认证
服务热线: 0571-86019278
电话 0571-86091936
总代理:浙江日丰工贸有限公司
Http://www.carpoly.com.cn
易施工、耐黄变。
低气味、干燥快。
裂纹漆：裂纹大小易控制，
装饰性好。
硝基漆
NC PAINT
欢迎光临
紫荆花专卖店:杭州中豪市场A区1010号 电话:0571-8696
2F 门 窗
1F 油漆、墙
圣丹漆
古象漆
圣丹漆 浙江涂料市场十大优秀品牌

九牧集团
美
加
华
中国卫浴专家
China's Bathroom Professional
服务承诺：
专卖地址：
电话：
立邦漆
木器漆 多乐士 墙面漆

新世纪装饰材料市场
新世纪装饰材料市场
饰城
活新天地
鳄鱼漆
杭州华利装饰装璜材料有限公司
上海海达建筑五金厂
家俱锁
公司地址：杭州市秋涛北路120号
开关
天创
咨询电话：

建材行业龙头市场
佳好佳居饰商城
向前
1000米
比品牌比价格 买的就是放心
宇辉酒家

佳成橱柜

杭州墙纸批零中心
dada
哒哒厨柜
4180元/套
装饰材料市场
墙纸
油漆
区
EUROART

场
86992324

佳好佳
质量担保 先行赔付
瓷砖卫浴
大卖场
瓷砖卫浴展示批发中心
向前50米
新多防撬门

中豪建材市场
中豪门窗城
地址：秋涛北路80号 电话：0571-86992324
向前50米
桑拿设备
电话：13082828341
上海万事诚厨饰有限公司
杭州直销处

好山、好水、好鸡
一"山沟沟"本鸡
红伟雕刻
"山沟沟"本鸡专卖店

孔雀大厦
OCEANO
天下无砖
元素·空间·服务
欧神诺陶瓷
新疆帕米尔餐厅
PAMIR RESTAURANT

浙江大学后勤集团主办
新型地板
装饰材料市
向前800
友谊石材
博亚橱柜

SIEMENS
mobile
我让黑暗如此美丽!
杭州天乐通信
杭州天乐通信器材有限公司
HANGZHOU TIANLE COMMUNICATION EQUIPMENT CO.,LTD

杭州汉和建材有限公司 客服中心：0571-86086011
东鑫泰酒店制服
施家山14号 电话：0571-56190515 13858089525

新
上
市
零度
可口可乐

买建材，到新型，我看行
非常促
行
86432042 86034088
KNAUF 可耐福
可耐福专卖店
杭州龙泰建材总经销
杭州龙泰建材经营部
星牌矿棉板
北京星牌建材有限责任公司
北京名牌产品
ISO9002质量体系认证

PART 5

URBAN CANVAS
AN IMAGE SPECTACLE
REPRESENTATIONAL AND NON-REPRESENTATIONAL
城市画布，影像景观——具像的与非具像的

中国作为一股经济力量的崛起，已促成了其国民和政治的历史转变。从一个蔑视财富、将财富视为洪水猛兽的社会，到一个褒扬甚至鼓励个人财富的社会，短短几十年发生的突变，确实给社会带来了不稳定因素。

文化大革命结束后，当中国国家领导人邓小平发布向外国资本和技术“开放”的政策时，他严肃地告诫百姓，“资产阶级思想的渗透是不可避免的”[59]。在整个20世纪80年代，反精神污染运动对于从烫发到西方文学的一切都实施了严格的限制。今天在中国，人们不得不承受着资产阶级（可以解读为西方引入的）思想、时尚和媒体的狂轰滥炸。从好莱坞大片到发型以及店里的商品，中国精神污染的指示灯早已亮起。可支配收入的迅速增长，使得这一局面更加复杂。杭州市统计局统计，2008年1月至10月，城市居民人均可支配收入超过两万元[60]，几乎是2003年的两倍[61]。对杭州居民来说，这些飞速增长的指数直接体现为一条生活方式进步和物质回报增加的轨迹。

杭州的街道就是一块画布，从发展中的农业社会到全球化消费导向型社会的戏剧性转变在这块画布上演绎出来。游击式的广告大战，刚刚涌现的婚庆业，无处不在的“美女凝视”，以及人造服装模特儿大军丰富了杭州充满活力的街头生活。都市画布寻求通过将具像（形象化或写实）从非具像（抽象、非形象化）的现象中区别开来，从而使这种混乱局面得到肃整，而这两个门类之间存在着相互转化的可能性。文化的渴望、活力以及假象模糊了任何直接的基准，而杭州也造就了她21世纪的新身份。

China's forceful rise as an economic power has incited historic shifts of its citizenry and politics. Transforming from a society where wealth was once scorned and considered an immoral force, to a society that commends, even encourages, personal affluence, within the short span of only a few years has certainly had destabilizing effects.

When Chinese Leader Deng Xiaoping decreed an "open door" policy for foreign capital and technology at the end of the Cultural Revolution, he somberly warned his people that "the penetration of bourgeois ideas is inevitable".[74] Throughout the nineteen eighties Anti-Spiritual Pollution campaigns implemented restrictions against everything from hair perms to Western literature. Today in China one cannot help but be bombarded by bourgeois (read Western imported) ideas, trends and media. From Hollywood DVDs to haircuts to products in stores, China's spiritual pollution barometer is on high. Rapidly growing disposable incomes have further compounded this situation. Hangzhou Statistics Bureau shows that from January to October 2008, the per capita disposable income of urban residents was over 20,000 RMB ($2941 USD), [75] this is almost double that of the amount in 2003.[76] For Hangzhou residents these hastily increasing figures translate directly into a trajectory of life style advancement and material reward.

The streets of Hangzhou are a canvas whereupon the dramatic transition from a developing, agricultural society to a globalized, consumer-oriented one plays itself out. Guerrilla advertising campaigns, a burgeoning wedding industry, a mosaic of printed pretty gazes and an army of mannequins populate Hangzhou's vibrant street life. The *Urban Canvas* seeks to codify this chaos by distinguishing representational (figurative or realistic) from non-representational (abstract, nonfigurative) phenomena and the possibility that these categories are interchangeable. Indexes of cultural desire, dynamism and simulacrum offer obscurity beyond any immediate reference as Hangzhou fabricates its new, 21st century identity.

WESTERNERS 西方人

URBANCANVAS

城市画布，影像景观——具像的与非具像的

基本而言，中国社会是单一文化的，汉族占绝对多数。尽管过去三十年来，中国经历了非华裔的突起（截至2004年，在中国生活居住的外国人估计达26万[62]），但仍然明显缺乏“他者”。这种缺失有一个例外——西方人以人造服装模特儿的形式充斥着杭州的大街小巷。中国商店里所使用的大部分模特儿，都是仿照西方人的样子。这些无处不在的形象，炫耀的表情有时显得诡秘，有时又显出令人难以忘怀的忧伤，本身就构成了一个族群。店主不仅在橱窗里陈列一两个这样的模特儿，而且在商店里摆出二三十个，有时候甚至开拓到店外的人行道上。这些模特儿的最早起源已无从知晓。有些人猜测，它们最初是从俄罗斯进口的，目前在本地生产。无论起源于哪里，它们如何代表中国消费者这一问题始终是个谜。如何把一个人的身份投射到一个与之看上去完全不同的物体上呢？这样的模特儿又如何成为中国普通消费者的代表呢？

尽管这些问题可能一直都找不到答案，但这些模特儿的面貌却借助于化妆、衣着和维护日益变得中国化了。尽管杭州的大部分服装模特儿仍然由西方人组成，但更新的、更现代的、有时甚至是卡通人物正开始取代它们。在今天的中国，像Lucky Human, Good Luck以及My Chance这类模特生产企业都在为国内外市场生产多文化的服装模特儿。杭州就有蓬勃的服装模特儿批发市场。

Chinese society, for the most part, is mono-cultural, with the Han Chinese leading by a fierce majority. Though China has witnessed a trickling in of non-Chinese over the last thirty years (as of 2004 there were an estimated 260,000 foreigners living in China[62]) there still remains an explicit lack of 'others'. This absence has one exception-Westerners are in abundance throughout Hangzhou in the simulated form of clothes mannequins.

The majority of mannequins used in Chinese stores are modeled on Western features. These ubiquitous figures, flaunting expressions that are sometimes quirky, other times hauntingly sad, constitute a population in itself. Stores owners will not just display one or two of these mannequins in the window but line the shop with an army of 20-30, sometimes even colonizing the sidewalk outside of the store. The origin of these models is unknown. Some hypothesize that they were originally imported from Russia and are now produced locally. Wherever they originated, the question of how they represent the Chinese consumer is a puzzling one. How to project one's identity onto something that looks nothing like oneself? How is the mannequin a surrogate for the average Chinese consumer?

While these questions may go unanswered, the faces of these models have become increasingly Chinese-fied through cosmetics, clothes and maintenance; and while Westerners make up the mannequin majority in Hangzhou, newer, more modern, sometimes even cartoony figures are beginning to replace them. In China today, model companies such as Lucky Human Mannequins, Good Luck Mannequin, and My Chance Enterprise all produce multi-cultural versions of clothes mannequins for both domestic and export markets. Hangzhou itself has its own thriving mannequin wholesale markets.

MEIBIAO

036

DRAGON

特卖场
时装内衣优惠价10元

花内衣
每件25元

Tailormade
woollen
clothes

88元/件

THE FEMALE GAZE 女性的凝视

URBAN CANVAS

城市画布，影像景观——具像的与非具像的

从一开始，广告业就始终把诱惑当作是市场营销的工具，不禁令人想到“性总是畅销的”这句古老格言。在中国，近三十年来广告业一直被一本正经的女性形象以及政府授权的宣传所把持，性主题的重新引入具有十分重要的意义。

2007年，当封面上刊登着性感歌手碧昂斯的《性感宝贝 – 泳装特刊》首次冲击报摊时，购买狂潮异常凶猛。但是这一年早些时候《男人装》就已经让难挡诱惑的中国男人动心了，封面刊登的是摆出一幅充满暗示的姿势、衣不蔽体的中国歌手阿朵的照片[63]。在中国大陆，这个主题仍然是个禁区，而色情照片是被中央政府所查禁的，那么这些杂志不仅具有高度的挑衅性，而且是一个真正的信号，即性主题正渗透到主流媒体中。

在杭州的整个商业影像当中，人们很快就可以识别出那些无处不在的特写头像，女性用直接的注视来诱惑观众。年轻漂亮的中国女模特盯视着观众，用固定不变的、充满诱惑的凝视将他们禁闭起来。从化妆品到笔记本电脑广告，这些直接的凝视反映出中国女性无畏而性感的实力。在广告业当中，传统上女性一直是被客体化的，而当下被凝视所抓住的却是观众，这使得观看和被观看都得以客体化了。这里，女性的凝视似乎是在利用甚至嘲弄男人的欲望。

这组照片还令人想到了中国女性面孔的另一些问题：日益严峻的男女比例失调（到2020年，婚龄男性将比婚龄女性多出三千万）[64]，卖淫业的稳步增长（据估计从一百万增加到一千八百万）[65]，性教育的贫乏，单身母亲等等，这些也是现代化的西方社会几十年来一直面对的问题。

Since its inception the advertising industry has always used seduction as a marketing tool, prompting the old maxim that “sex sells”. In China, where for almost 30 years the advertising industry was substituted by entirely prude, state administered propaganda, the reintroduction of sexual themes is significant.

When *Sports Illustrated’s* swimsuit issue hit the newsstands for the first time in 2007, flaunting the sexy singer Beyoncé on the cover, the buying competition was fierce. But earlier that year *For Him Magazine* had already wet the palettes of China’s lusty men, with a cover that featured the barely dressed Chinese singer, A Duo, in a compromising position.[63] In mainland China, where the subject is still taboo and pornography is outlawed by the ruling Communist Party, these magazines are not only highly provocative, but also a true sign that sex is infiltrating mainstream media.

In commercial imagery throughout Hangzhou one can quickly identify a dense pattern of close-up images where women seduce the viewer with direct eye contact. Pretty, young Chinese models stare out at the viewer locking them in a fixed invitational gaze. Advertising everything from cosmetics to laptop computers, these direct stares reflect a courageous, sexual empowerment of the Chinese female. In the advertising industry where woman are traditionally objectified, it is the viewer in this case that is caught in a staring game, objectifying both observed and observer. Here the female gaze seems to exploit, almost mock male desire.

This set of images also summons other issues that woman face in China: the increasingly lopsided male to female ratio (By 2020, there will be some 30 million more men of marriage age than women)[64], the steady rise of prostitution (estimates vary from 1 to 18 million)[65], poor sexual education, single motherhood and other problems that the modernized West has been dealing with for decades.

51697383

51697383
51697383

美容胶囊
让

MAY

UL

"未来掌握在我手中"
LUX
时空美白
SHISEIDO
动人的眼睛会
双效焗油
我的
PARIS

Canon

WEDDING INDUSTRY 婚庆业

URBAN CANVAS

城市画布，影像景观——具像的与非具像的

婚庆业是中国发展最为迅速的行业之一。官方统计数字表明，每年大约有一千万对新人登记结婚，婚庆花费高达2,500亿元[66]。随着生活标准的提高，出于对豪华婚礼的热衷，专业人士找到了一个有利可图而且增长异常迅猛的巨大市场。一家婚庆策划公司指出，他们组织的大部分豪华婚礼的花费都在130万元左右，而普通婚礼花费大约在7,000元，这是杭州人平均月工资收入的2.5倍[67]。2006年是中国人认为吉祥的年份，婚礼数量增加了50%[68]。当在线游戏《都市2046》在国庆节长假期间（这是中国最受欢迎的婚礼举办日之一）为游戏参加者提供特别婚礼服务时，结婚甚至在虚拟世界中也流行起来。但这仍无法同2008年8月8日相比，在这个由三个8组成的日子里，有三十万个婚礼共享着北京奥运会开幕式的聚光灯[69]。

杭州也从婚庆行业的增长中获益非浅。位于风景如画、充满传奇色彩的西子湖畔，杭州以被称为“中国最浪漫的城市”而自豪。这里有很多民间传说，讲述恋人们在著名的西子湖畔幸福快乐、与鬼怪斗争或化为蝴蝶的故事。2006年，杭州关于爱情的传说吸引了来自全国各地的一百三十对新人，他们在该市举办的婚礼促销活动上集体举行婚礼。根据行业分析，影楼和附属设备供应占婚庆市场的25%至40%[70]。杭州的婚庆店和工作室最近还运用了倍受争议但却方兴未艾的裸体婚纱照，大胆开发其浪漫的布景。尽管这种有伤风化的婚纱照片令很多人震惊，但也有人盛赞这个日益增长的现象是“在恢复一个陈旧却永恒的传统”[71]。

The Wedding industry is one of the fastest growing industries in China. Official statistics show that approximately 10 million couples register to marry annually in China and spend some 250 billion yuan (US$30 billion) on their weddings.[66] With rising living standards, combined with a craze for extravagant weddings, professionals have found a huge, lucrative and quickly growing market. One wedding planner cites the most expensive wedding they organized at 1.3 million yuan (US$157,000) with the average wedding costing a more sober 7,000 yuan (US$933 or two and a half times the average monthly wage in Hangzhou).[67] 2006, a year that was believed to be particularly auspicious by the Chinese, saw a 50% increase in the amount of marriages.[68] Marriages even became popular in the virtual world when the online game *City 2046* offered a special wedding service for players during National Day Weekend, one of the most popular times for a wedding in China. But this is nothing in comparison to August 8, 2008 whose lucky triple eight date saw a record 300,000 weddings share the spotlight with the opening of the Beijing Olympics.[69]

Hangzhou has reaped many benefits of the wedding industry's growth. Owing to the picturesque and legendary West Lake Hangzhou boasts itself as being China's most romantic city. There are several folktales about lovers whom frolic, battle with ghosts or turn into butterflies around the famous lake. In 2006 Hangzhou's amorous legacy attracted one hundred and thirty couples from all over China who got married concurrently in a city sponsored marriage promotional event. According to an industry analysis, photo studios and peripheral suppliers occupy 25 to 40 percent of the wedding market.[70] Hangzhou's wedding boutiques and studios have certainly exploited their romantic setting, most recently with the controversial but growing popularity of nude wedding photos. While this risqué brand of wedding photography has shocked many, others welcome the growing phenomenon as a "renewal to the stale, unchanging tradition".[71]

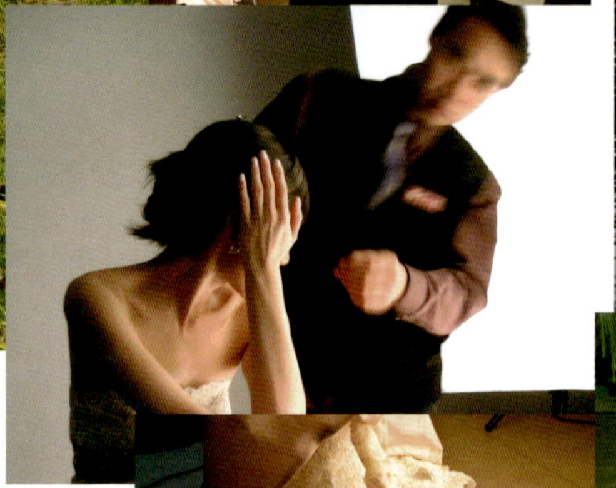
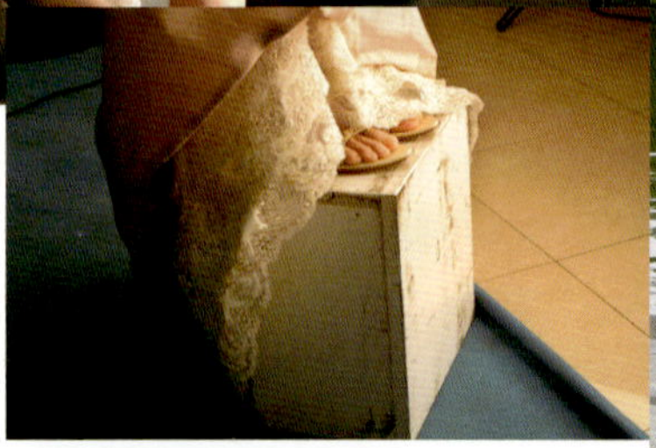

手座
PHOTO
STUDIO
写真摄影
MARKSMAN PHOTO
個性婚紗攝影

中波摄影
2007 世界海景主题
演绎极尊浪漫
ZBO
RAREZONE
稀园 文艺摄影会馆
10年
感恩大回馈
婚纱摄影

AB-EX, BAN ZHENG
抽象表现主义，办证
URBAN CANVAS
城市画布，影像景观——具像的与非具像的

不论外电报道多么糟糕，中国仍存在着一个专门涉及版权侵权、知识产权侵权以及其他侵权行为的行业，它不仅是个出口行业；而其普遍存在也使得这个国家处于在自己“家”里也要不断重申真实性的尴尬境地。

在中国的各个城市，知识侵权犯罪分子在到处进行着汪达尔式、游击式的市场促销。办证可以直译成“办理证件”。但是在杭州的公共场所，“办证”其实是在为伪造证件作宣传。一位警官指出，一个人从生到死所需要的全部证件，都可以通过拨打这些广告电话得到：结婚证、驾驶证、营业执照、身份证、土地证、文凭甚至军官证[73]。按照新华社的报道，广州30%的资格证和12%的文凭都是伪造的[74]。在中国，声称拥有学历的人数比合法授予文凭的人多出50万，这不禁让人心中充满疑惑[75]。有一个此类办证公司声称自己雇佣了一万人，而哈尔滨市从事清除广告垃圾的工人竟与此相等[76]。

这类广告垃圾由一个手机号码和“办证”两个汉字组成，涂写在围墙、大门、过街天桥甚至整个城市的标志牌上。这些广告是非法的，不仅因为提供了可疑的服务，而且损坏了公共财产。环卫工人、警察和（或）被抓获的犯罪者用建筑油漆和刷子涂掉这些标志。往往油漆尚未干透，手机号码就又被写在上面，而不断涂和写的过程就这样继续下去。这种来来回回的对话营造出一种丰富的审美语言，令人想起1960年代美国式涂鸦、抽象表现主义以及那些波普艺术家们（克莱因、罗森伯格、德库宁、罗斯科、汤布里等等）。

中国飞速的城市化和经济强权地位的崛起，留下了众多有趣的裂隙，而当一个国家的执法机关也被重重包围的时候，会发生什么呢？一位办证工人这样描述此种形势：“只有当社会进步到道德觉醒的地步时，才不再会有我们的容身之地”[77]。与此同时，假证件的需求也相当之高，就像媒体所称的，这种“城市牛皮癣”将继续出现在中国的城市画布上。

In spite of bad foreign press, China's industry in copyright infringement, intellectual-property violations, and other infractions of authorship is not only an export business; it is an enterprise whose pervasiveness puts the country in the awkward position of continually reassessing authenticity at home.

In China's cities the domestic intellectual crime industry is most visible in its vandalistic, guerilla style marketing campaigns. 办证 *ban zheng* directly translated means to 'make certificates'. But on Hangzhou's public surfaces 办证 *ban zheng* are the characters that advertise the production of false documents. One police officer observed that all the documents one needs from birth until death are obtainable by responding to these ads: marriage, driver's, and business licenses, identity cards, land deeds, diplomas, even army officer ID badges.[73] According to Xinhua News agency: 30% of qualification certificates and 12% of all diplomas in Guangzhou were found to be fake.[74] Suspicions also arose when the number of people claiming to hold degrees in China turned out to be more than 500,000 higher than the number of diplomas legally awarded.[75] One such *ban zheng* company claims to employ 10,000 people, while the city of Harbin has an equal amount of workers dedicated to cleaning up this illegal advertising mess. [76]

This mess consists of a cell phone number and the characters, 办证 scrawled over walls, doors, overpasses, and signs throughout the city. The ads are illegal not only for providing suspect services, but also for the defacement of public property. Community sanitation workers, police and/or the caught perpetrators sloppily cross out the marks with house paint and brushes. Often, cell phone numbers are then re-scrawled atop this fresh drippy surface and the layering continues. This back and forth dialogue creates a rich aesthetic language reminiscent of both American style graffiti tagging and the abstract expressionists and pop artists of the early 60's (Kline, Rauschenberg, DeKooning, Rothko, Cy Twombly, etc.).

China's speedy urbanization and rise to economic-superpower status has left behind many interesting ruptures, but what happens when a country's organs of legitimization have been circumvented? One *ban zheng* worker described the situation this way: "Only when society has advanced to a point of moral enlightenment, will there no longer be room for us".[77] In the meantime, demand for false documents is high, and this "urban psoriasis", as the press has termed it, will continue to abstract China's urban canvases.

work in Hangzhou
创业在杭州
住在杭州
游在杭州
39196933
办证
施工单位
NRG
安瑞吉
接待会
13166162313
办证

13136101855
北
The
办证 刻章
办证 刻章
谢晋
话: 64313308
15825529886
13391950355
办证
献血 救人之义举
上海五月天
SHANGHAI MAY GARDEN

创建安全
小区，人人有
责，人人参与。
新华路街道综治办、派出

有电危险
请勿靠近
电子
网易NETEASE
www.163.com
用我们的双手

Synthesis
必须戴好安全帽
复路98号
中共江干区

13391918137
13366827272
13011883329

HANGZHOU-ERS 杭州人

URBANCANVAS

城市画布，影像景观——具像的与非具像的

本书试图在这个构建得充满活力的环境之中，阐释真实的人。杭州大约有七百万人口，与美国芝加哥和洛杉矶市人口之和相当，是中国人口第十二大的城市。她吸引着周边省市的移民前来工作、投资和娱乐。像每个城市一样，在杭州，各种不同类型的角色每天在上演着这座城市的大型生活戏剧，正如他们所居住的大楼和那些招牌，杭州人身上印着时代变迁的痕迹。衣服、饰品、发型和气质不仅标志着日益全球化的环境，也是个体适应和个人诠释的生动体现。这些图片描绘的无数个体正构成了杭州的城市人口学。

Amongst the vibrant constructed environment that this project seeks to illustrate are actual human beings. Hangzhou has a population of almost seven million, about the metropolitan size of Los Angeles and Chicago combined. It's the twelfth most populous city in China, attracting migrants from surrounding provinces and beyond for work, investment and pleasure. Like every city there are all types of characters that act in the grand opera of daily life, and like the signs and buildings that they inhabit, the people of Hangzhou bear the mark of changing times. Clothes, accessories, hairstyles and habits become mobile signifiers not just of an increasingly globalized environment but also of individual adaptation and interpretation thereof. The images here depict the myriad of personalities that compose the demography of Hangzhou.

IMPOSSIBLE IS NOTHING

集散中心
招商处
饭店
招商处
24

PART 6

MARKETS INSIDE/OUT
市场内外

广告最终走向了市场。在中国，自文化大革命结束以来，集贸市场也经历了不断扩大的过程。1980年代的时候，如博物馆一般的国营百货商店以及杂乱无章的露天农贸市场成为中国人购物经验的典型例证。今天，杭州人有着和美国没有多少区别的令人眼花缭乱的多种购物选择：特定商品的购物城、跨国超市及时装连锁店、出售名牌折扣品和出口转内销原单产品的精品店、多姿多彩的报亭、规模庞大的批发市场、隐蔽的DVD商店以及网吧，它们一起为人们提供了多样的选择。而真正丰富的不仅仅是店铺，还有店铺内外的店铺。杭州主干道旁的人行道上，到处是提供促销活动和表演的帐篷和舞台，也提供了商店内部不具备的便利。在大商场内的某些角落里还存在着出售非法盗版DVD的商店。小心翼翼地坐落在商店上层的网吧，为“自我一代”的无数青少年提供了避难之所。这些出生在1980年代之后缺少兄弟姐妹的孩子们，体现了中国的独生子女政策，也代表了驱动着众多市场的新型消费热潮。

The road of advertisements eventually leads to the market. In China the marketplace has undergone a process of continual magnification since the end of the Cultural Revolution. During the 1980s official, museum-like department stores, and unruly, open-air flea and food markets typified the Chinese shopping experience. Today a dizzying array of shopping options, not unlike the U.S., exists for Hangzhouers. Mega-stores, multinational supermarkets and fashion chains, small boutiques that sell name brand knock-offs and off-the-truck originals, multicolored magazine stands, colossal wholesale marts, covert DVD shops, and Internet Bars help to quantify one's available options. Not only are there stores galore but there are also stores within and outside of stores. On the sidewalks of Hangzhou's main strips are colonies of tents and stages offering marketing events, performances and oddly, the convenience of not being in a store. Illegal, bootleg DVDs are sold in stores that are burrowed within the framework of larger stores. Internet Bars, discreetly situated above stores provide havens for millions of youngsters that compose the 'me generation'. This generation of sibling-less children born post-1980 personify both China's one child family policy as well the burgeoning consumer frenzy that drives these many markets.

MAGAZINE STANDS 报亭

MARKETS INSIDE/OUT
市场内外

五花八门的报亭在杭州的各个角落里旗帜鲜明地宣告着自由世界的到来（或者至少是关于自由世界的八卦和趋势）。截至2007年11月，中国出版了大约9468种期刊杂志，年总产值达到170亿元[78]。这一增长的绝大部分归功于中国媒体市场向国外期刊的开放，实际上取代了国内一万一千多种资金匮乏的共产主义期刊。为努力使媒体合理化，北京新闻出版署于2003年宣布，将不再要求共产党员订阅由国家部委和地方政府出版的那些内容浮夸老套的报纸和杂志。很多期刊停办了，而同时又有数千种期刊转而出版流行刊物[79]。

今天，除了有中国字以外，杭州的报亭看起来与巴黎和纽约的报亭没有什么区别。《计算机世界》、《网络世界》、《国家地理》 以及 《个人电脑》 都出售中文版。自2000年以来，《财富》、《福布斯》以及《哈佛商业评论》都加入到中国的商业杂志期刊领域，另外数种期刊，例如《美丽佳人》、《时尚》、《ELLE》、《虹》、《现代新娘》以及《时尚芭莎》也在诱惑着这个国家有时尚意识的都市女性，更不用说数千种中国的期刊杂志不断冲击着中国出版业的界限。

1980年代早期西方颓废思潮的侵袭使得政府相信，是时候关上大门了。而今天，已经没有回头路了。

Kaleidoscopic magazine kiosks brightly announce the coming of the free world (or at least the free world's gossip and trends) from every corner in Hangzhou. As of November 2007, 9,468 magazine titles were published in China generating about 17 billion yuan (2.29 billion U.S. dollars) in total annual output value.[78] Much of this increase is due to opening the Chinese media market to foreign titles, which has virtually replaced the country's 11,000 cash-strapped communist periodicals. In an effort to rationalize the media sector, Beijing's General Administration of Press & Publications announced in 2003 that it would no longer require Communist Party members to subscribe to many of the turgid, grey newspapers and journals published by ministries and municipalities. Many periodicals closed, while thousands of others converted to publishing popular titles.[79]

Today, except for Chinese characters, newsstands in Hangzhou do not look that different from those in Paris or New York. Computerworld, Network World, National Geographic and PC Magazine all sell Chinese editions. Since 2000, Fortune, Forbes, and Harvard Business Review have joined the field of Chinese business magazines, and more than a dozen titles such as Marie Claire, Vogue, Elle, Madame Figaro, Modern Bride, and Harper's Bazaar are wooing the country's fashion-conscious urban women, not to mention the thousands of Chinese titles which are increasingly pushing the boundary of what is publishable in China.

In the early 1980s the inroads of Western decadence persuaded the government that it was time to start closing the door. Today there is no turning back.

科幻世界
消费电子世界 3元赠送你册
消费电子世界
CONSUMER ELECTRONICS WORLD
游戏在MP4里
走进MID的世界
手机中的双枪将
2007
为游戏选
手机服务听
大众医学
家庭用药
自我保健
新财富
兵器知识
舰载武器
销售与管理
时尚健康
钱规·钱关
MONEY
读《心理月刊》更好地生活
心理 PSYCHOLOGIES
品位
世界时装之苑
ELLE
50
圣诞新年
贴心礼物
PUBLIC BUSINESS INTELLECTUAL
寻求亚洲的变革力量
东方企业家

華夏地理
发现最老的婴孩
全球候鸟迁徙

她世纪她时尚的引领者

INTERNET BARS 网吧

MARKETS INSIDE/OUT
市场内外

网吧是另一种全新的空间，伴随着中国经济改革和开放政策而涌现出来。网吧通常位于购物中心或街边小店的二楼，这些满是尘埃的避风港为大众提供上网服务。成排的计算机，多数键盘上的字母已经因为频繁的使用而磨光了，为沉迷于游戏的中国年轻一代提供了避难所。虽然大部分这类场所有年龄限制，但消费者年龄仍从12岁到35岁不等。大部分顾客是家里没有电脑，或被禁止过度使用电脑的人，或者是没有其他途径上网的农民工。在网吧里，顾客们玩着在线游戏、观看下载的电影、加入聊天室或者听音乐等等来打发时间。这是一个在虚拟世界里，有时过度频繁地联系在一起的群体。很多家长和有关部门已经开始警惕上网成瘾的过度蔓延，年轻人牺牲了学业、营养甚至睡眠来享受上网之乐。据一份报告说，一位母亲在无法成功地限制自己儿子沉溺于网络后，试图自杀[80]。今天，全国制定了几项计划，旨在改善沉溺网络的现象。

2006年，中国的互联网用户每周大约花费20亿小时上网，而美国用户登录时间仅为1.29亿小时。中国还有着巨大的增长空间。2006年，美国活跃地使用互联网的用户占美国人口的一半，而中国则占总人口的11.7%[81]。从2003年至2008年，中国的互联网正式用户从1.78亿人猛增到2.53亿人[82]。按照这一增长比率，沉迷于网络的现象未来无疑将在中国继续蔓延。

The 网吧 *wangba* or internet cafe is another newly fashioned space that has emerged along with China's policies of economic reform and opening up. Usually situated on the second floor of shopping centers or strip malls, these dusty havens offer the service of getting online. Rows of computers, many with their keyboards wiped clean from incessant use, offer refuge for China's game hungry youth. While most of these tucked away venues have age limits, customers vary anywhere from 12 to 35 years old. Most of the patrons either don't have computers at home, are forbidden from using them with such surfeit, or are migrant workers with no access to the internet otherwise. In Internet cafes, clients idle away their time playing online games, watching downloaded films, participating in chat rooms, listening to music stations, etc. It is a group that communes in the virtual world, sometimes way too often. Many parents and authorities have become alerted to an epidemic of Internet addiction wherein teens sacrifice studies, nourishment and sleep for the pleasure of being online. According to one report a mother even attempted suicide after unsuccessfully trying to curb her son's addiction.[80] Today there are several programs throughout the country aimed at reforming this addiction.

In 2006 Chinese Internet users spent nearly two billion hours online each week, while the U.S. audience logged on for only 129 million. China also has a lot more room to grow. While roughly half of the U.S. population was actively using the Internet in 2006, just 11.7% of the Chinese population was plugged in.[81] From 2003 to 2008 regular Internet users in China grew by 178 million to 253 million.[82] At this rate of growth Internet addiction will undoubtedly haunt China in the future.

在线网吧
中国工商银行
停车收费

众骐网吧
大安网盟
网吧
文林超
公话超市
各品牌电板配件

順興駿業

禁止吸烟

禁止

MARKET PERFORMANCE 促销表演

MARKETS INSIDE/OUT

市场内外

随着中国经济的增长以及中国人口袋里可支配收入的充足，市场促销变得越发具有攻击性，甚至公共空间如今也成为潜在消费者的围猎场。在杭州，促销活动定期在热闹的购物中心前面的人行道上举办。往往一座用彩印帐篷搭建的临时建筑、精心设计的大棚和舞台占据了原本用作其他目的的公共空间。舞蹈、音乐、化妆舞会、互动游戏、抽奖、时装表演以及喜剧表演吸引着购物人群和天真的路人。小有名气的电视主持人、歌手或演员频频出现，帮助介绍和促销产品。新闻媒体通常也受到邀请，有时候甚至通过礼品和贿赂被劝说到商场参加活动或推销产品。除表演之外，那些搭在公共场所的帐篷成为方便购物者了解并且购买物品的路边小店。这些“速卖店”或“商店之外的商店”不仅提供了便利，而且吸引着完全没有购物意愿的消费者。露天的购物和活动场所在一个十几年前非官方的公开聚会或商品的庆祝仪式都被禁绝的国家具有惊人的效力。

As China's economy grows and disposable incomes fill Chinese pockets, marketing has become increasingly aggressive, to the point where public spaces are now stalking grounds for potential customers. In Hangzhou, marketing events are held on the sidewalks in front of popular shopping destinations on a regular basis. Often a temporary architecture of printed tents, elaborately designed booths and stages occupy the otherwise public space. Dance, music, and COS Player performances, interactive games, raffles, fashion shows, and comedy acts draw the shopping crowd and innocent passersby. Semi-famous television hosts, singers or actors are frequently employed to help launch or promote products. The press is usually invited and sometimes even persuaded, through gifts and bribes, to run stories about the event and/or pitched product. Besides performances, tents are often erected in the public domain, operating as small sidewalk boutiques where shoppers can sample, learn about and purchase the items at hand. These 'summary stores' or 'stores outside of the store' not only offer convenience but also attract customers who had no intention of shopping at all. Exterior shopping and event sites have been surprisingly effective in a country where non-official public gatherings and the celebration of material goods were banned not so long ago.

位于地下商场
飞越2006
杰奥
羽绒服十大影响力品牌
杰奥羽绒服形象代言人张铁林
12月16日下午1:30驾临 杭州解百
解百集团
ESTĒE LAUDER
三得利
新口味
新登场
TCL
王牌
今天进入未来
超薄机身 如卡随行
M810

欢欣鼓舞
元华周年庆典
4

周年庆

动感
时尚
随我炫
NEC手机 N1XX系

电信手机商场请上三楼

牌
铁林
州解百
上城保
BA
中国 浙江

贩可去
元华4F
恒源祥 邀您与羊共
瞬间紧致我颜的秘密
KENWOOD
Hello KittyHello Kitty
神田
SUNING
至真至诚 阳光服务
WWW.CHINADQ.COM
欢
KOOKAÏ
罗莱家纺05婚庆推广暨秋冬产品热卖会
元华店庆开幕了!
满1200元减585元
满800元减390元
满400元减195元
我的世界 炫酷元界
四驱车电视大赛(海选)
不准泊车
NO PARKING

中国名牌
国家免检
Juanna
富安娜
Camel
Australia
Tussah
Australia
SPRUCE
Richcel Quilt
Australia
SALE

CARS AND COFFEE 汽车和咖啡

URBAN CANVAS

市场内外

随着全球市场增加了在中国的投入，杭州西湖周围出现的两种现象体现了就品味和身份而言的文化同化过程——汽车与咖啡。

中国的文化特征是同五千年来的饮茶传统紧密结合的。杭州也素以西湖龙井而闻名，这种中国最著名的绿茶在全国乃至全世界都受到消费者的青睐；有些人甚至认为这是中国的国饮。尽管大部分杭州当地文化都与之有关，但城市也面对着另一种带有文化色彩的饮品出现，那就是咖啡。今天，咖啡馆林立在风景如画的南山路以及西湖充满田园诗意的步行街两侧。在西湖景区主要入口的边上生意兴隆的有星巴克、哈根达斯、考斯塔咖啡、牙买加咖啡以及世家蓝迪咖啡吧。按照星巴克中国区总裁王金龙的说法，中国的咖啡消费每年稳步增长25%。截至2007年，星巴克在全国有246家分店（其中10家在杭州），很明显这个国家不久将成为其最大的海外市场[83]。

虽然咖啡为中国的茶文化提供了另一个选择，还有一种奇特的机构也林立在西子湖畔，与咖啡全球化的成熟需要相呼应：那就是豪华汽车经销店。从法拉利、陆虎到宾利等等各种品牌盘踞在著名的西湖周围，兜售他们的产品。百万富翁的人数每年增长20%，2008年已高达40万人，豪华汽车市场并没有显示出衰退的迹象。德国汽车制造商奥迪在中国售出了101,996辆汽车，不仅首次突破10万辆大关，而且超过了它在美国的销售量。中国也是奔驰最畅销的S-Class的第二大市场[84]，而2007年保时捷、法拉利以及宾利在中国的销量都翻了一番[85]。正如咖啡一样，豪华汽车也是显示消费者地位、国际化和品味的战利品。

While the global market flexes its muscles in China two manifestations around Hangzhou's West Lake point to processes of cultural homogeneity in terms of taste and status.

China's cultural identity is bound together with its 5000-year tradition of drinking tea. Hangzhou is known for its famous Dragon's Well or *Longjing* Tea. *Longjing*, China's most famous green tea is consumed throughout the country and world; some even regard it as the national drink of China. While much of Hangzhou's regional culture revolves around this bountiful resource, the city faces the growing presence of another, culturally charged drink: coffee. Today, coffeehouses line the idyllic Nanshan Road as well as the West Lake's bucolic pedestrian walks. Standing in formation at one of the Lake's main access points are a Starbucks, Haagen-Dazs, Costa Coffee, Jamaica Coffee and Segafredo Zanetti. According to Starbucks China President Wang Jinlong, coffee consumption in China has risen steadily at 25% per year. Starbucks, which as of 2007 has 246 outlets in China (10 of which are in Hangzhou), projects that the country will soon be one of its biggest overseas markets.[83]

While coffee offers an alternative to China's tea culture, another curious set of establishments also line the West Lake and echo coffee's sophisticated cry for globalization: luxury car outlets. Every brand from Ferrari to Land Rover to Bentley has staked out territory around the prestigious West Lake to vend their goods. With the amount of millionaires growing at 20% annually, topping 400,000 in 2008, the luxury-car market is showing no signs of slowing. German car-maker Audi sold 101,996 vehicles in China, not only breaking the 100,000 barrier for the first time, but also the amount of its U.S. sales. China is already the No. 2 market for Mercedes' best-selling S-Class[84] and Porsche, Ferrari, and Bentley all doubled their sales in 2007.[85] Like coffee, luxury cars are trophies that signify the consumer's status, worldliness and taste.

也不曾以560匹骏马开路。
一全新宾利欧陆 GT 轿跑车
BENTLEY
BENTLEY HANGZHOU
宾利杭州

APPROPRIATE PARKING
P
专用车位
APPROPRIATE PARKING
P
专用车位

MINI CLUBMAN
BMW授权经销商：
浙江金湖
销售热线：0571-88860077
地址：杭州市文一西路508号
浙江金湖城市展厅
销售热线：0571-28990099
地址：杭州市西湖大道333号

Mercedes-Benz

BENTLEY
利杭州 英国宾利汽车授权代理

PORSCHE

PORSCHE

Ferrari

MASERATI

Mercedes-Benz

100%Expectation

贝尼尼咖啡
Bernini
贝尼尼咖啡
COFFEE PUB

BLUE MOUNTAIN CAFE

1 酒全楼
2 云·水 餐厅酒吧
3 Segafredo 世家兰迪咖啡吧
5 哈根達斯 Häagen-Dazs
6 ★ STARBUCKS COFFEE ★
7 花酒年代
8 VA BENE 华缤霓
9A 湖蝶 餐厅
9B 福林堂 新一代
9C 西湖天地专卖店 The Xihu Tiandi Gift Shop
10 西湖翡翠花园酒家 Xihu Crystal Jade Garden Restaurant
11 COSTA COFFEE
12 牙买加咖啡 Jamaica
15 西湖天地服务中心 Xihu Tiandi Service Center

维莎咖啡
Le varza CAFE

迪欧咖啡 DIO COFFEE
迪欧 咖啡
DIO COFFEE

咖啡
Coffee
南山路
185

摩卡咖啡南山店
WESTERN RESTAURANT

STARBUCKS COFFEE
Häagen-Dazs

C. straits cafe

THE GREAT DVD TRADE 卖碟

MARKETS INSIDE/OUT

市场内外

尽管政府对盗版DVD的销售进行了打击，但是盗版行业在中国继续肆意膨胀。虽然打击被视为仅仅是安抚外国电影公司和政府，但盗版DVD的消费已经成为中国当代文化的一部分，为很多人提供了电影、外国电视、游戏和音乐方面的二手教育。从尚未公开发行的好莱坞大片，到完整的《黑道家族》、《六人行》或者《越狱》这些电视连续剧，到《国家地理》特别节目和最新的文艺片，再到佛列兹·朗、希区柯克、伯格曼、戈达尔和帕索里尼的经典之作，看似无限的丰富多样使得中国转入了对全球流行文化的狂热之中。外国制作并非版权侵权的唯一受害者。中国的电影制作人也控告中国的电视台每年公开播放1500部盗版中国电影，给中国的电影公司造成了高达940万美元的收入损失[86]。这些统计数字之外，事实上盗版电影占国内电影市场的90%，这对中国电影工业来说实在是一场灾难[87]。

不管中国的知识产权面临何种危机，盗版DVD的销售在中国很多城市都是公开进行的，有时光天化日之下就在大街上兜售。像杭州这样的地方受到了较多管制，这里对盗版DVD生意的处罚是初犯罚以一万元，再犯往往有可能导致牢狱之灾[88]。但这往往仍无法阻止该行当的存在。经销商缩小了规模，退到隐蔽的地方，常常是在电子市场里。这些商店中的商店环境完全是实用而简陋的，商品陈列在纸板箱里或者挂在墙上。这种隐蔽的暗箱操作通常是由前店的店员来做广告，虽然显露出其非法行为，但仍然逃过了政府机关的视线范围。还有一些经销商则出现在夜幕里，在露天跳蚤市场或便利店边上兜售自己的货品。

Despite routine crackdowns on the sale of pirated DVDs, the bootleg industry in China continues to boom. While crackdowns are seen as simply placating to foreign film studios and governments, the consumption of pirated DVDs has become part of contemporary Chinese culture, providing many with a second hand education in film, foreign television, gaming and music. Everything from yet unreleased Hollywood thrillers to the complete *Sopranos, Friends,* or *Prison Break* television series; to National Geographic specials and the latest art house favorites; to classics like Fritz Lang, Hitchcock, Bergman, Godard and Pasolini, the seemingly infinite variety has turned many Chinese into savvy aficionados of global popular culture. Foreign productions are not the only victims of copyright infringement. Chinese filmmakers also accuse Chinese TV stations of airing up to 1,500 pirated Chinese movies a year, costing Chinese movie studios up to $9.4 million in lost revenues.[86] These statistics coupled with the fact that pirated films occupy over 90% of the domestic market spell disaster for the Chinese film industry. [87]

Regardless of China's impending copyright bankruptcy, the sale of pirated DVDs happen overtly in many Chinese cities, sometimes on the street in broad daylight. Other places like Hangzhou are more regulated. Here punishment for bootleg DVD peddling is a mandatory RMB10,000 ($1470 USD) fine for a first-time offense, while repeat offenses can often result in incarceration.[88] However this usually doesn't deter business. Instead the dealer retreats to smaller, closeted spaces, usually within electronic or computer markets. These stores within stores are totally practical, spartan environments, with merchandise displayed in cardboard boxes or hung on the wall. The covert back room operations are usually advertised by the front room staff, which reveal the illicit activity, but still keep it out of authority's sight. Other merchants emerge under the cover of night and vend their goods at outdoor flea markets or on the sides of convenient stores.

瑞星杀毒软件
RISING ANTIVIRUS Personal Edition
主动防御 · 即时升级 2008
DEXTER
Optical Wheel House

杭州仟仟电脑商行
K3121
海牛插座

参加大抽奖!
赢得笔记本
COMPANY OF HEROES
PTC Pro Engineer
HEALING HANDS

GAEL GARCIA BERNAL
THE SCIENCE OF SLEEP
科学睡眠
GEORGES DE BEAUREGARD PRESENTE
JEAN SEBERG
JEAN-PAUL BELMONDO
A bout de souffle
筋疲力盡
dans un film de JEAN-LUC GODARD
JEAN-LUC GODARD
La fille d
d'Artagn
豪情玫瑰
THE DREAMER
戏梦巴黎
UN FILM DI BERNARDO BERT
dts
LES CHORISTES
放牛班的春天
THE CRITERION COLLECTION
通往绞刑架的电梯
LOUIS MALLE'S
ELEVATOR TO THE GALLOWS
m'aime

SUPER MARKET 超市

MARKETS INSIDE/OUT

市场内外

从小型街边售货亭、“便利店”到巨大的“电脑城”，杭州的商业活动全面出击，试图将资本主义狂潮包容在内，呈现出多种外观和规模，一个比一个更大。

杭州有742家日用品和批发市场[89]，其中很多兼作为购买廉价品的零售店。这些市场的年交易额达到2310亿元[90]，与此相伴的是市场外街道上喧嚣的景观。市场里，迷宫一样的走廊上堆放着将要发出和收到的货品，成为交货人、货车以及顾客实现渴望的一条无止境的通道。这些市场当中，很多人经营服装和服装配件，成为该市最主要的出口商品之一，按照香港贸促会的说法，这使得杭州成为“女装之城”[91]。

杭州的另一类超级商场就是“购物城”，这些购物城是由多层分布的独立摊位组成的。组成这些特种市场的许多摊位，出售着各种同样的产品。在杭州，独立的购物城主要包括照相录像器材、电脑产品、电子设备、五金器材或者上述商品的大杂烩。尽管这些地方已经被产品和人拥挤得水泄不通，但广告仍然充斥着残余的空间。在楼梯的正面，墙上，从天花板上悬挂下来，或者是立在一旁的展板，广告无处不在。

第三类大型商店也入住杭州——仓储式零售超市和百货连锁店。这些商店提供的数量消费模式近年来迅速发展起来。杭州的主要国内和国际连锁店包括：联华、华联、乐购、家乐福、麦德龙、百安居、易初莲花以及沃尔玛等等。

From modest street kiosks to ‘summary stores’ to the colossal ‘Computer City,’ commercial activity in Hangzhou is full blown. The spaces that attempt to contain the frenzy of capitalism come in a variety of shapes and sizes, one out-supersized by the next.

Hangzhou is home to 742 commodity and wholesale markets,[89] many of which double as retail outlets for bargain shoppers. The RMB 231 billion (34 billion USD)[90] worth of annual trade that these markets see is accompanied by a spectacular cacophony on the streets outside. Inside, a labyrinth of hallways, stocked with outgoing and incoming orders, funnels an endless procession of delivery men, carts and browsers to their desired destinations. Many of these markets deal in garments and clothing accessories, one of the city’s major exports, which according to the Hong Kong Trade Development Council helped to name Hangzhou the “city of women’s wear”.[91]

Another type of mega store in Hangzhou is the item-specific ‘shopping city’. These ‘cities’ take form as an expansive collection of independent booths spread over multiple levels. The many cubicles, which compose these specialized markets, sell variations of the same products. In Hangzhou independent shopping cities exist for photography/video gear, computer products, electronic equipment, hardware, or a bargain basement mishmash of all the above. While these environments are already jam-packed with products and people, advertisements fill in the remaining space. On the fronts of stairs, plastered on walls, hanging from the ceilings, or as self-standing cutouts, advertisements are everywhere.

A third category of mega-store also inhabits Hangzhou- the warehouse retail outlet and department chain stores. The mass consumptive modes that these stores offer have been developing at a fast pace in recent years. Major national and international chain stores in Hangzhou include Lianhua, Hualian, Hymart, Carrefour, Metro, B&Q, Lotus, Trustmart, etc.

舒适保
PHYSICAL
Cyber-shot
自有我主张
HANDYCAM
分享快乐
如此简单
DSC-T9
T9 超级光学防抖
数码相机
SONY
SONY
华
清
新科移动DVD专卖
PHILIPS
Micro
SAMSUNG
TCL
Splendid
靓彩显示引擎
华硕靓彩显示

PHYSICAL
Canon
60GB大容量
SONY
Canon
FUJIFILM

Verbatim 威宝
TDK

万"纤"风情
全球至薄

Nelac
移动你的心
Canon
IXUS

三星 mp3 mp4
T9 想象 无线自由
ASUS
华硕品质·坚若磐石
丽屏靓影
双核先锋
才够配
Cyber-shot
新色彩的IXUS,你的

NOKIA
NOKIA
NOKIA
NOKIA

Canon

anon
我的DV
是佳能
108分钟
光盘记录 • 220万像素
宜静宜动
PhotoDV
数码单反相机
EGO 西溪数码港
买数码 到西溪
做中国数码第一店
Nikon

Z5
yepp'
IT.com.cn 权威推荐

飞时达 电动车
FAST E-BIKE
休闲生活 从此开始!
Easy Life From Fast E-bike

0571-88821203\13738172999

大白鲨
电动自行车
到知
永多
远年
动力强劲

绿源
开宝马 坐奔驰 骑绿源电动车
奔豹电动车
德国技术 高新科技
奔豹电动车

真的很专业!
程序电机
超强动力

杭州爵帅
爵帅电动车
OKOK

新英雄
杭州

诚品
信牌
直相
到知
永多
远年

爵帅
Shuai
著名节目主持人

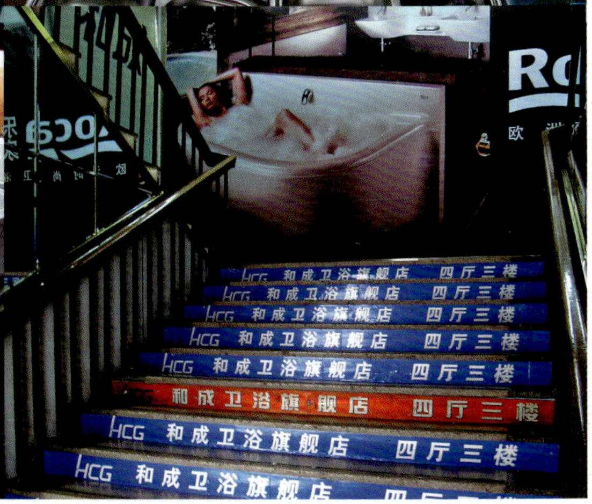
HCG 和成卫浴旗舰店 四厅三楼

ART NO.
COLOUR
SIZE
QTY
21件

METRO
圣诞快乐 喜迎2007
Merry Christmas Happy new Year

物满68元即
获得一个积点,
买多送。
ENTRANCE

PROMOTION
无购物出口
NO PURCHASE
无购物出口
NO PURCHASE
EXIT
积点成
特价
PROMOTION

PROMOTION
特价 特价
PROMOTION PROMOTION
特价 特价
银鹭
花生牛奶

出口
EXIT

特价 PROMOTION
¥49.90

YOUREACH
又衣栈
CUTIE
女星潮爆

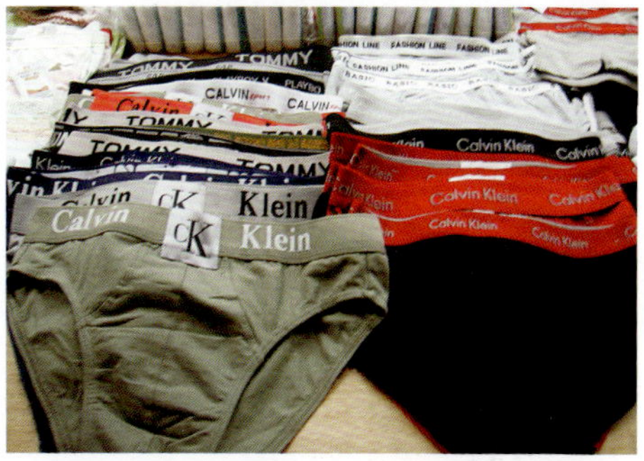
TOMMY
Calvin Klein

一律2元/件

DANGER
PEMCO

WHITE BOX

EPILOGUE:

While *Learning from Hangzhou* attempts to analyze the urban semiotics affected by China's momentous economic development it concentrates, and is born out, of an infatuation with signs. That is signage everywhere. In this sense it could've also been "Learning from Omaha" or Manila or London or the many other cities of the world permeated with outdoor signage. Furthermore much of what is indexed in this book also exists in the West. The idea is not to present what is novel, but on the contrary, to codify what is ubiquitous and subsequently what has become invisible to us. At the core of this project is repetition, reoccurrence. Even though I cannot erase my own subjectivity from these observations what I have re-presented here is visual proof of omnipresent urban phenomena in Hangzhou; in text I have tried to illuminate the signification of these phenomena in the context of today's China. That being said, the billboards, the architectural eclecticism, the water dispensers, air conditioner units, etc. are as much Hangzhou's as they are part of a global urban topography. While this book is a micro case study it simultaneously speaks about the entire world.

Hangzhou is, and is perceived as, a beautiful, idyllic and traditional city. Though it may not be explicitly conveyed in this book – I adore Hangzhou, its slow pace, lush surroundings and air of cultural self-confidence. For the past five years I have enjoyed going back and forth to Hangzhou, plying further into its ever changing physicality and reaping the pleasures of its warm hospitality. Yet it was Hangzhou's tranquility that, for me, made an even more convincing case for examining the influence that real estate opportunism and the advertising industry has upon a city. Beyond the placid and romantic West Lake that Hangzhou is known for, the city possesses all the anarchic attributes of a developing city caught in the frenzy of economic expansion. The contrasts presented here counter the romantic perception of the city while at the same time posing a warning for the future. China's recent economic and urban growth is indeed historical and awesome. But what is the endgame? What will be the social and environmental toll? In ten years time what will be Chinese and what will be attributes of a global culture? What will this even mean in 10 years? How does a city manifest the cultural shifts of its populace? These are things that I have tried to observe and encapsulate, as a document of a moment in one city's evolution, for both China and the rest of the world. I have made the publication bi-lingual and distributed it in China deliberately to participate in the open, ongoing discourse about urban development in China (and elsewhere) for all of those involved and affected, especially for those whose sense of familiarity has clouded the obvious.

In 2003 when I went to The China Academy of Art's New Media Department as an artist/professor in residence I had been to the city only one time before as a tourist. However, I wasn't new to China, having lived in Beijing from 1994-1998. Since first coming to China I was obsessed not only by its advertisement and propaganda signs but by the signs of its rapid sociocultural changes as well - by the semiotics of its urban centers per se. China's codes were, and still are, in a state of continual flux. No two readings of the place can be the same. It is a condition that keeps one looking, and I kept looking at China's signs.

But in fact my infatuation with signs was not only limited to China. New York City, where I have called home for most of my adult life, is an exemplar outdoor signage site. The Pulaski Bridge overlooking the Long Island Expressway as it enters the midtown tunnel into Manhattan is one of my favorite sign spotting points, similar to the Shanghai-Hangzhou-Ningbo highway in this book. There is also Broadway and Lafayette in Soho with its towering, sexy fashion ads and, of course, the apex of sign sites- Times Square where you feel that you are literally walking through a huge three dimensional electronic magazine. These sign-cluttered environments had in fact inspired a series of site-specific billboard projects that I had been working on in the United States and which I wanted to bring to China. My billboard artworks use photography as a way to inquire about the effects that sign structures and images have on personal space, the public domain, perception, cognition, memory and the architectural surroundings as well. Each of these billboard works consisted of a photographic image taken in the area in which it was placed. The idea was to create a self-referential and receding space, similar to trompe l'oeil painting, rather than an ad which projects outwards. Furthermore every site and corresponding image was chosen as a way to index the social or political relevance of that particular site. For instance there was a work located near the former World Trade Center in New York City shortly after the incidences of 9-11, other works addressed water pollution, politics, gentrification, or the infestation of other surrounding outdoor signage.

When I came to the residency in Hangzhou I began to seek out an appropriate location for my next billboard project. In investigating the possibilities I was amazed at the scale and quantity of billboards that the city offered. I began recording the different types and configurations of Hangzhou's outdoor signage. In my exploration I also noticed the myriad of architectural styles that the city possessed and other ubiquitous signs of social-cultural change. I began recording these as well. The idea was that these photos were to assist me in deciding where and how I would mount my next site-specific billboard piece. Everyday I would bicycle around the city photographing, looking, learning. Patterns began emerging in my growing archive of photographs. Categories led to more categories. The city began to be deconstructed into its component parts and slowly my photographic catalog took on a life of it's own. While I had already located a potential site for my billboard project, and began negotiations with the brokering agent, my photographic collection still kept growing.

At the same time I was reading *Learning from Las Vegas* which is a book about signs and the semiotics of architecture and cities. Even though this book was written over thirty years ago its relevance was still strong, especially when I visited the wholesale district in what, at the time, was still considered the suburbs of Hangzhou. It was here that the link was made. These buildings were completely wrapped, head to toe, in signs! They were buildings that were signs and signs that were buildings. It was then that I really started Learning from Hangzhou.

For me this book is a both a celebration and a critique of this energized and expanding city. If, in the end, it poses more questions than it answers, that is, like the Italo Calvino quote I used in the opening, precisely the experience of visiting a city that lies beneath a thick coating of signs- However the city may really be... whatever it may contain or conceal, you leave Hangzhou without having discovered it.

后记

《向杭州学习》试图分析受中国全力以赴加速经济发展的影响的城市符号学，以及由此而生的对标牌的痴迷。标牌无处不在。在这个意义上，它也可以是"向奥马哈学习"，或者马尼拉、伦敦及世界上充斥着户外标牌的许多城市。不仅如此，更多编入本书中的内容也存在于西方世界。目的不是猎奇，正好相反，是编纂普遍存在的和因此让我们视而不见的东西。这个计划的中心便是重复与再现。虽然我无法消除自己的偏见，但这里再现的便是杭州具普遍性的城市现象的视觉证明；而文字部分我试图说明这些现象的重要内涵。或者说，广告牌、建筑的折中主义、饮水机、空调等等既是杭州的，也是世界城市地志。而本书虽是一个微观的个案研究，探讨的却是整个世界。

杭州被视为田园诗般传统而美丽的城市。尽管这点在书中没有明确表达——我热爱杭州，它庸懒的节奏、苍翠繁茂的环境和文化上的自信风范。在过去的5年里，我一直很快乐地往返于杭州，定期往返于其不断变换的外表，并享受它的热情好客。而对我来说，是杭州的宁静，使它成为检验房地产投机者和广告业对一个城市影响的更有说服力的例证。除了使其闻名遐迩的平静浪漫的西湖，杭州还具有因为经济扩张的狂热而给这个发展中的城市带来的混乱特质。在此所呈现的削弱了它的浪漫，也给未来敲响了的警钟。中国最近的经济和城市发展的确是具历史性和异乎寻常的。它的尾声将是什么？其社会和环境的牺牲是多少？10年后，中国以及世界文化的特征将是什么？而这些10年后又意味着什么？一个城市又如何表达其百姓的文化变迁？在一座城市不断前进的某个时刻，这些都是我努力观察和总结的，为中国也为西方。我有意将这本书以双语形式出版并在中国发行，以参与到正在进行着的关于中国（及其它地方）的城市发展，与相关的和受影响的人们展开开放对话，特别是为那些由于太熟悉而"不识庐山真面目"的朋友。

我在2003年作为艺术家和客座教授访问中国美院新媒体系之前，只到杭州旅游过一次。但中国对于从1994至1998年已在北京生活过的我来说并不陌生。自从第一次来中国，使我着迷的不仅是它的广告和宣传标牌，还有社会文化飞速变化的标记——属于都市本身的符号。中国的代码曾是、始终是不断变迁的状态。两次去同一个地方是不会一样的。这是一个另人百看不厌的状态，而我也在一直观察着中国的标牌。

但实际上我对标牌的迷恋并不仅限于中国。在我度过大部分成年时光的家乡纽约市，就是户外标牌地的典范。朴拉司基桥上眺望长岛高速路转入中城隧道而进入曼哈顿，是我最喜欢的标牌的观景台，与本书中提到的宁沪杭高速类似。同时SOHO区的百老汇和拉法叶大街屹立的性感的时装广告，当然还有标牌聚集地的登峰造极之作——时代广场，在那里你会觉得你真的是漫步于巨大的三维电子杂志之中。堆放在一起的标牌环境正是我在美国的一系列广告牌作品的灵感来源，我想把这个作品也带到中国。我的广告牌艺术作品运用照片来考察标牌构筑物和形象对于个人空间及公共的场所、感受、认知、记忆和建筑环境的影响。更进一步，每一个广告牌作品，包含着在所在场地拍摄的照片，目的是为了创造一种自我指设的后退空间，类似于错视画，而非广告的外向投射。而且每一个地点与其对应的图片都是根据该场地的社会与政治关系加以选择的。比如，911事件发生后不久的一件作品就坐落在911遗址旁，其他作品表达了水污染、政治、优化改建，或者其他附近户外标牌的侵扰等。

住在杭州时，我开始为下一个广告牌计划寻找合适的地点。在考察这种可能性时，我为这座城市所提供的广告牌的规模和数量惊诧不已。我开始纪录不同种类和布局的杭州户外标牌。在我的探索中，还发现这座城市拥有的大量各种建筑式样及其他带有普遍意义的社会文化变迁的迹象，对此我也开始进行纪录。拍的这些照片只是为了帮我决定下一个"特定场地"广告牌作品的地点和固定方式。我每天骑着自行车满城跑：拍照、观察、学习。模式开始在不断增加的图片档案中形成。一个种类变成更多种类。城市开始解构成它的各个组成部分，渐渐地我的摄影画册有了自己的生命。在我已经为自己的广告牌计划找到了可能的场地，并开始与房地产中介协商的同时，我的摄影集也在不断地扩大。

同时我正在读《向拉斯维加斯学习》，一本关于标牌、建筑与城市符号学的书。尽管这本书写于30年前，它依旧很适宜，尤其是在我参观批发区，当时被认为是杭州的郊区的时候。关联就此建立起来。这些建筑物被标牌从头到脚的包裹起来。建筑物就是标牌，标牌就是建筑物。从那一刻起，我开始向杭州学习。

对我来说，这本书是对这座生机勃勃地扩张中的城市的祝贺和评析。如果到最后它带来了比答案更多的疑问，正如我在开头引用的伊塔罗•卡尔维诺所述的那样，非常准确地：拜访一座隐藏在厚实的标牌下面的城市的经历，不管城市到底怎样，它包含或隐藏了什么，你已经一无所获地离开了杭州。

公区

24小时
营业

鸣谢:

本计划受资助于格雷姆美术高等研究基金会。

在他们的帮助下，这本书的出版才成为可能：张大力、亚洲文化协会、张培力、中国美院新媒体系、杨燕、王小峰、克拉瑞萨•迪亚兹、帕玛拉•朱、彼得•波力塞维其、詹姆斯•波尔立和BAU Architecture、王澍、章建明、盛建华、吴蔚、朱涛

特别感谢：彼得和玛丽•波力塞维齐、克李斯托夫•菲力浦斯、罗波特•伯奈尔、谢文跃、纽约艺术与建筑画廊、缇牟和艾伦•万浩森、丹尼尔•乌夫塞尔、克李斯廷•波力塞维齐、马克•拉菲亚、吴美纯、郑为民和东大名创库。特别是杨燕，一直相信着我，在这个费力耗时的努力过程中始终是我不断的灵感来源和支持。

非常感谢杭州和杭州人，尽管我展示的可能不是一座美丽城市的最美丽的一面，但他们曾是并仍然是我持续不断的灵感来源。

ACKNOWLEDGEMENTS:

This project was supported with a grant from the Graham Foundation for Advanced Studies in the Arts.

Without the generous assistance of the following persons and institutions this book would not have been possible: Zhang Dali, Asian Cultural Council, Zhang Peili and The China Institute of Art's New Media Department, Yang Yan, Wang Xiaofeng, Clarisa Diaz, Pamela Jue, Peter Borysevicz, James Brearley and BAU (Brearley Architects and Urbanists), Wang Shu, Zhang Jiangming, Sheng Jianhua, Azure Wu and Zhu Tao

Special Thanks to: Peter and Mary Jo Borysevicz, Christopher Phillips, Robert Bernell, Xie Wenyue, Storefront for Art and Architecture, Tim and Ellen Van Housen, Kerry Scheidt, Marlaine Glicksman, David Shadrack Smith, Daniel Wolfskehl, Kristian Borysevicz, Marc Lafia, Wu Meichun, Zheng Weimin and DDM Warehouse, and especially Yang Yan who believed in me and was a continuous source of inspiration and support through this very laborious and time intensive endeavor.

A very special acknowledgement to the city and people of Hangzhou who, despite that I showed what may be considered the not-so-pretty side of this very pretty city, were and are a source of continuous inspiration.

文章注解

序

1 俗语
2 陈述彭，《杭州的城市扩张》，中科院2002年长江三角洲发展国际研讨会
3 杭州统计信息（2008年12月10日），人口总量部分，参看杭州统计信息网http://www.hzstats.gov.cn/webapp/show_news.aspx?id=18177
4 香港贸易发展委员会（2007年11月），《中国各省份和城市市场概况》， http://info.hktdc.com/mktprof/china/hangzhou.htm
5《杭州人口十年内增长100万》，参看人民网2001年4月16日，http://english.peopledaily.com.cn/english/200104/16/eng20010416_67832.html
6《中国城市数量达到665个》，人民网2008年11月5日，http://english.people.com.cn/90001/90776/90882/6528090.html
7 吴娇（音） “2020年前中国５０％的人口会是中产阶级,” 中国日报, 2007年12月27日
8 罗伯特・文丘里、斯蒂文・依泽诺 和丹尼斯・斯科特・布朗，《向拉斯维加斯学习：建筑形式被忘却的符号》，美国麻省理工学院出版社1972年版，麻省剑桥，1977年修订版，第1–190页

Italo Calvino 引述
Italo Calvino, 看不见的城市. Tr. William Weaver. 伦敦: Vintage, 1972,1997

拆与建：重复循环

9 陈述彭，《杭州的城市扩张》，中国科学院2002年长江三角洲发展国际研讨会
10 庄洪涛,《周宇鹏：长江三角洲城市扩大与加速发展》摘自《人民日报》网络版 2007年9月15日
11 麦克斯・图侬，《中国的劳动力内部迁移：特征与反应》，国际劳工组织，2006年4月，第10页
12 研究与市场部，《2006年中国房地产市场投资分析报告》，研究和市场，奥尔巴赫国际公司，2007年7月
13 宁越敏，《长江三角洲地区：城市化与大城市改造》，香港中文大学第四届人口地理学国际研讨会，2007年7月10–13日
14《中国的建筑》，《经济学家》杂志，2005年3月10日
15《住房保障的“杭州模式”》，《杭州日报》2007年9月14日
16《市场需求决定房价走势 杭州非理性时代终结》，《楼市》2008年06期
17 潘家华，《建设节约型社会》，中外对话，2007年11月5日
18 阿瑟・路波,《中国综合症》 纽约时报, 2006年5月21号
19《2007年末及2008年长期规划报告》杭州市规划局（2008年1月），参看http://www.hzplanning.gov.cn
20《豪华住宅广告牌是房价居高的替罪羊吗？》，《北京周报》2007年6月14日第24期，参看http://www.bjreview.com.cn/forum/txt/2007-06/13/content_65997.htm

建筑的折衷主义

21 与作者的对话，阳光海岸公寓，2008年12月1日，杭州
22《历史沿革》，杭州市人民政府，2008年，www.hangzhou.gov.cn
23 同上引文
24 与杭州市政规划局西湖分局副局长章建明的谈话，2006年11月18日，杭州
25 2008年国际文学节上，保罗・安德鲁2008年3月9日在上海米式西餐厅对一个提问作出的答复
26 与建筑师王澍的对话，2006年11月20日于杭州中国美术学院。同济大学被认为是中国最优秀的建筑和城市规划学府之一，其课程范围最为全面
27 与建筑师王澍的对话，2006年11月20日于杭州中国美术学院
28 与澳大利亚BAU建筑与城市设计事务所建筑师詹姆斯・布莱利（James Brearley）的对话，2008年12月3日，上海
29 风水是一种基于道教信仰的古代占卜术，相信大地是有生命的，拥有“气”或能量。通常这种方法被用于确定建筑物、周围空间以及建筑物内部陈设的位置，以便确保健康、财富和好运
30 人口统计数额
31《现代性：国际化风格》，梅尔默－迈克来因管理公司，2008年
32 查理斯・詹克斯与艾伦・兰克，《建筑的现代运动》，（伦敦企鹅艺术与建筑丛书，1973年版）
33 滨江房产集团陈晓峰与作者的对话，阳光海岸公寓，2008年12月1日，杭州
34 谭克蒙（译音），《大转折》，《建筑》杂志2006年第2期第8卷，90–96页
35 与杭州市政规划局西湖分局副局长章建明的对话，2006年11月18日，杭州
36 与建筑设计师王澍的对话，杭州中国美术学院，2006年11月20日
37 与建筑设计师王澍的对话，杭州中国美术学院，2006年11月20日
38 国家统计局《2003年中国统计年报》及《2008年中国统计年报》（中国统计出版社）
39 李申（译音），《探究中国住房价格上涨》，中国网2007年9月1日，www.china.org.cn
40 滨江房产集团陈晓峰与作者的对话，阳光海岸公寓，2008年12月1日，杭州
41 风水和逻辑的规律：朝南意味着阳光可以全天照射. 这两种法则使得居室朝南在客户的需求当中名列首位
42“钱塘江南岸新城”，（2006年10月），参看http://www.hzdjy.com/english/hz.asp
43 滨江房产集团陈晓峰与作者的对话，阳光海岸公寓，2008年12月1日，杭州。《2008年中国统计年报》（中国统计出版社）
45 滨江房产集团陈晓峰与作者的对话，阳光海岸公寓，2008年12月1日，杭州

建筑中的行为

46《有毒的河流和焦渴的城市》，引自《中国的环境健康和水质恶化》，中国环境论坛，参看http://www.wilsoncenter.org，2008年12月
47 乔纳森·瓦兹，《水边》，英国卫报2004年11月11日， http://www.guardian.co.uk/environment/2004/nov/11/water.china
48《长江三角洲面临污染危机》，中国日报2005年9月26日
49《中国饮用水市场调查报告》，研究与市场，2008–2009年， http://www.researchandmarkets.com/research/317fcd/china_drinking_wat
50《中国仍在建设“耗能过渡”的建筑》，中国日报2008年1月14日
51《降低中国能源消耗：关于建筑调试鲜为人知的事实》，中国企业社会责任新闻，2008年7月21日， http://www.chinacsr.com/en/2008/07/21/2523-keeping-energy-costs-down-in-china-little-known-facts-about-

作为建筑物的广告牌/作为广告牌的建筑物：广告的幽闭症效应，从微观到宏观

52《中国广告业预测报告，2007–2010年》， 研究与市场，奥尔巴赫国际咨询公司，2007年5月
53 金玉米，《人力资本与中国新兴的广告和媒体行业》，单位网，2005年12月9日
54《杭州社区实施地方交通警示》，法制日报2006年6月9日
55《政府与行业讨论中国汽车市场的未来》，中国汽车行业发展国际论坛，2005年
56 与杭州市政规划局西湖分局副局长章建明的谈话，2006年11月18日，杭州
57 与杭州市政管理办公室的对话（该局批准杭州市的所有广告许可），2008年12月29日
58 这个想法取自《向拉斯维加斯学习》，该书谈到拉斯维加斯已成为建筑物外观的精致广告。“波罗迷尼纽店和意大利宫酒店巴洛克式的外观成为了同样出类拔萃的经过装饰的大棚”。《向拉斯维加斯学习》，第107页

城市画布，影像景观—— 具像的与非具像的

59 皮科·耶尔，大卫·艾克曼，北京报道，《抵制精神污染》，时代周刊，1983年11月
60《前十个月居民人均可支配收入突破两万元》，2008年11月20日，杭州市政府办公信息处理中心http://www.hangzhou.gov.cn/main/zpd/English/CityNews/T269176.shtml
61 2003年，人均可支配收入为1558美元。亚当·罗斯，维薇安·方，《一座古都有信心取得高技术腾飞》，中国经济评论2004年9–10月
62 “外国人喜欢在中国居住和旅游。” 新华社， 2004年10月4日
63 大卫·巴尔博扎，《中国的一场人民性解放》，纽约时报2007年3月4日
64 王珊珊（音译），《三千万男性将单身面对孤独的未来》，中国日报2007年1月
65 同上引文
66《婚庆革命席卷中国》，人民日报，2004年10月
67《婚庆行业在中国兴旺起来》，全国妇女联合会，2005年5月
68《白头偕老——七万元的价格》，上海星报，2006年8月17日
69《中国刷新奥运婚礼纪录，30万对新人于08／08／08喜结良缘》，新华社2008年8月9日
70 同上引文，注释68
71《裸体婚纱照成为中国一大新趋势》，中国日报，2006年3月13日
72 同上，中国国家统计局
73《北京查获假证制作和销售假证五万件》，北京青年报，2002年5月14日
74《欺骗是一种地方病吗？》，中国日报BBS，2004年5月
75《假文凭成为一种流行病》，国际先驱论坛报，2002年10月15日
76《谁能治愈中国城市的牛皮癣？》，世界经理人文摘，2007年5月18日
77 腾达证件网，2008年12月，《辉煌的未来》，www.tdzjw.org

市场内外

78 宋书涛（音译），《中国报刊杂志数量激增》，新华网《中国评论新闻》2007年11月17日
79《外国杂志引起中国报摊热潮》，商务周刊，2003年11月5日
80《沉迷互联网男孩令母亲轻生》，中国日报，2005年9月23日
81《中国互联网用户超过美国》，福布斯杂志，2006年4月刊
82《亚洲互联网的使用与人口》，尼尔森评级，2008年
83《星巴克从中国采购咖啡》，路透社，2007年9月4日
84 布来恩·布来牟那《中国的豪华汽车：全速前进》，商务周刊，2007年4月19日
85 薇薇安·金，《豪华轿车在中国热销》，初探汽车网，2007年12月21日
86《电视台被控电影盗版》，深圳日报，2006年8月15日
87《盗版电影大大损害了国内电影行业的制作能力》，中国法治新闻，2006年6月28日
88 盗版DVD卖主同作者的对话。杭州颐高数码市场，2006年11月
89 2008年杭州统计年报
90 同上引书
91《中国省份和城市市场概况》，香港贸促会， http://info.hktdc.com/mktprof/china/hangzhou.htm

NOTES

INTRODUCTION

1 Traditional Saying.
2 Chen Shupeng, "Hangzhou Location Expansion," Chinese Academy of Sciences International Conference On Yangtze Delta Development 2002.
3 "Demographic Amount," http://www.hzstats.gov.cn/webapp/show_news.aspx?id=18177.
4 "Market Profiles on Chinese Cities and Provinces," Hong Kong Trade Development Council, http://info.hktdc.com/mktprof/china/hangzhou.htm, November 2007.
5 "Hangzhou's Population Increases One Million in Ten Years," People's Daily Online, http://english.peopledaily.com.cn/english/200104/16/eng20010416_67832.html, 16 April 2001.
6 "The Number of Cities in China Reached 655," People's Daily Online, 5 November 2008.
7 Wu Jiao, "50% of People to be Middle Class by 2020," China Daily, 27 December 2007.
8 Robert Venturi, Steven Izenour, and Denise Scott Brown, Learning from Las Vegas: The Forgotten Symbolism of Architectural Form, (Cambridge MA: MIT Press, 1972; 1977 Revised Edition).

Italo Calvino, Invisible Cities. Tr. William Weaver. London: Vintage, 1972,1997

DEMOLITION / CONSTRUCTION: CYCLES OF REOCCURRENCE

9 Chen Shupeng "Hangzhou Location Expansion," Chinese Academy of Sciences International Conference On Yangtze Delta Development 2002.
10 Zhuang Hongtao, "Zhou Yupeng: Yangtze River Delta Urban Expansion Quickens Pace and Improves Development," People's Daily Online, 15 September 2007.
11 Max Tuñón, "Internal Labour Migration in China: Features and Responses," ILO Office, 10 April 2006.
12 "China Real Estate Market Investment Analysis Report 2006," Research and Markets, Auerbach International Inc. July 2007.
13 Ning Yuemin, "Yangtze Delta Region: Urbanization and Megapolis Restructuring," The Chinese University of Hong Kong 4th International Conference on Population Geographies, 10-13 July 2007.
14 "Architecture in China," The Economist, 10 March 2005.
15 "Housing Security's 'Hangzhou Model'," Hangzhou Daily, 14 September 2007.
16 "The Market Needs to Decide the Housing Price, Hangzhou's Era of Irrationality is Over," Housing Market Journal, June, 2008.
17 Pan Jiahua, "Building a Frugal Society," China Dialogue, 5 November 2007.
18 Arthur Lubow, "China Syndrome," The New York Times, 21 May 2006.
19 Hangzhou Urban Planning Bureau, "2007 Year's End and 2008 Long Term Planning Report," http://www.hzplanning.gov.cn, January 2008.
20 "Are Luxury Housing Billboards the Scapegoat for High House Prices?," Beijing Review No. 24, http://www.bjreview.com.cn/forum/txt/2007-06/13/content_65997.htm, 14 June 2007.

ARCHITECTURAL ECLECTICISM

21 Conversation with the author, Sunshine Coast Apartments, Hangzhou, 1 December 2008.
22 "Historical Evolution," Hangzhou City People's Government 2008, www.hangzhou.gov.cn.
23 Ibid.
24 Conversation with Deputy Director Zhang Jianming, Hangzhou City Planning Bureau West Lake Branch, Hangzhou, 18 November 2006.
25 Paul Andreu in response to a question at the 2008 Literary Festival, M on the Bund, Shanghai, 9 March 2008.
26 Conversation with architect Wang Shu, China Academy of Fine Arts, Hangzhou, 20 November 2006.Tongji University is regarded as one of the best schools for Architecture and Urban Planning in China
27 Ibid.
28 Conversation with James Brearley, BAU Brearley Architecture and Urbanists, Shanghai, 3 December 2008.
29 "Fengshui" –literally wind,water- is an ancient geomantic practice based on the Taoist conviction that the earth is alive and possesses qi or energy. It has commonly been used to position buildings, the spaces around them, and the contents within them to assure health, wealth and good fortune.
30 Ibid 28.
31 "Modernity: The International Style," Mermel and McLain Management, 2008.
32 Charles Jencks and Allen Lank, Modern Movements in Architecture, (London: Penguin Art and Architecture, 1973).
33 Chen Xiaofeng of Binjiang Real Estate Group in conversation with the author, Sunshine Coast Apartments, Hangzhou, 1 December 2008.
34 Tan Kok-Meng, "The Big Shift," Archis No.2 Volume 8, 2006, 90-96.
35 Conversation with Deputy Director Zhang Jianming, Hangzhou City Planning Bureau West Lake Branch, Hangzhou, 18 November 2006.
36 Conversation with architect Wang Shu, China Academy of Fine Arts, Hangzhou, 20 November 2006.
37 Conversation with architect Wang Shu, China Academy of Fine Arts, Hangzhou, 20 November 2006.
38 China Statistical Yearbook 2003; China Statistical Yearbook 2008, National Bureau of Statistics of China, (China Statistics Press).
39 Li Shen, "In Depth: China's Housing Price Hike," www.china.org, 1 September 2007.
40 Chen Xiaofeng of Binjiang Real Estate Group in conversation with the author, Sunshine Coast Apartments, Hangzhou, 1 December 2008.
41 Both the laws of Feng shui and logic- southern facing means a full day of sunlight- have made southern exposure utmost on clients' list of demands.
42 "New Town South of Qiantang River," http://www.hzdjy.com/english/hz.asp, October 2006.
43 Chen Xiaofeng of Binjiang Real Estate Group in conversation with the author, Sunshine Coast Apartments, Hangzhou, 1 December 2008.
44 China Statistical Yearbook 2008. National Bureau of Statistics of China, China Statistics Press.
45 Ibid 43.

THE PERFORMATIVE IN ARCHITECTURE

46 "Toxic Rivers and Thirsty Cities," Environmental Health and Water Degradation in China, China Environmental Forum, http://www.wilsoncenter.org, December 2008.
47 Jonathan Watts, "On the Waterfront," The Guardian, http://www.guardian.co.uk/environment/2004/nov/11/water.china, 11 November 2004.
48 "Yangtze River Delta Faces Pollution Crisis," China Daily, 26 September 2005.
49 "China Drinking Water Market Report," Research and Markets, http://www.researchandmarkets.com/research/317fcd/china_drinking_wat, 2008-2009.
50 "China Still Building 'Energy-Guzzling' Buildings," China Daily, 14 January 2008.
51 "Keeping Energy Costs Down In China: Little-Known Facts About Building Commissioning," China CSR News, http://www.chinacsr.com/en/2008/07/21/2523-keeping-energy-costs-down-in-china-little-known-facts-about-building-commissioning/, 21 July 2008.

SIGN AS BUILDING/BUIDLING AS SIGN: ADVERTISING'S CLAUSTROPHOBIC EFFECT, MICRO TO MACRO

52 "China Advertising Industry Forecast 2007-2010," Research and Markets, Auerbach International Inc., May 2007.
53 Jeremy Goldkorn, "Human Capital and China's Rising Advertising and Media Industries," Danwei Media, 9 December 2005.
54 "Hangzhou Community Implements Local Transportation Guards," Legal Daily, 9 June 2006.
55 "Government and Industry Discuss the Future of China's Automotive Market," The International Forum of China Automotive Industry Development, 2005.
56 Conversation with Deputy Director Zhang Jianming, Hangzhou City Planning Bureau West Lake Branch, Hangzhou, 18 November 2006.
57 Conversation with Hangzhou City Office for Urban Management, 29 December 2008. The bureau approves all sign permits in Hangzhou.
58 This idea is taken from the book, Learning from Las Vegas which talks about the elaborate signs of Las Vegas that become the façade. "The Baroque facades of Borromini and the Italian palace is the decorated shed par excellence," Learning from Las Vegas, p.107.

URBAN CANVAS: AN IMAGE SPECTACLE - REPRESENTATIONAL AND NON-REPRESENTATIONAL

59 Pico Iyer and David Aikman-Peking, "Battling 'Spiritual Pollution'," TIME, November 1983.
60 "The Per Capita Income of Urban Resident Exceeded 20000 Yuan in The First 10 Months," Hangzhou Official Information Transaction Center, http://www.hangzhou.gov.cn/main/zpd/English/CityNews/T269176.shtml, 20 November 2008.
61 Adam Ross and Vivien Fang, "An Ancient Capital is Poised to Make a High-tech Leap," China Business Review, September-October 2004. In 2003 the per capita disposable income was 1,558USD.
62 "Foreigners Enjoy Living, Traveling in China," Xinhua News Agency, 4 October 2004.
63 David Barboza, "A People's Sexual Revolution in China," New York Times, 4 March 2007.
64 Wang Shanshan, "Thirty Million Men Face Bleak Future As Singles," China Daily, January 2007.
65 Ibid.
66 "Wedding Revolution Sweeps China," People's Daily, October 2004.
67 "Wedding Industry Flourishes in China," All-China Women's Federation, May 2005.
68 "Happily Ever After-With a 70,000 Yuan Price Tag," Shanghai Star, 17 August 2006.
69 "China sets Olympics wedding record as 300,000 couples tie knot on 08/08/08" Xinhua News Agency, 9 August 2008.
70 Ibid, 68
71 "Naked wedding photos a new trend in China," China Daily, 13 March 2006.
72 Ibid, National Bureau of Statistics of China.
73 "Beijing Flushes Out the Manufacture and Sales of 50,000 Fake Certificates", Beijing Youth Daily, 14 May 2002.
74 "Is Cheating Endemic?," China Daily BBS, May 2004.
75 "Diploma Forgery Becoming an Epidemic," The International Herald Tribune, 15 October 2002.
76 "Who Will Cure China's Urban Psoriasis?," World Executive Digest, 18 May 2007.
77 Tengda Zhengjian Wang, "Bright Future", www.tdzjw.org, December 2008.

MARKETS INSIDE OUT

78 Song Shutao "China Reports Growing Number of Magazine Titles," China View, 17 November 2007.
79 "Foreign Magazines Facing China's Newsstand Fever," BusinessWeek Magazine, 5 November 2003.
80 "Internet-addict Boy Drives Mother to Suicide," China Daily, 23 September 2005.
81 "China Surpasses U.S. In Internet Use," Forbes, April 2006.
82 "Asia Internet Usage and Population," Neilson Ratings, 2008.
83 "Starbucks to Source Coffee from China," Reuters, 4 September 2007.
84 Brian Bremner "Luxury Cars in China: Pedal to the Metal," Business Week, 19 April 2007.
85 Vivian Jin, "Luxury Cars Boom in China," Edmund's Inside Line, 21 December 2007.
86 "TV Stations Accused of Film Piracy," Shenzhen Daily, 15 August 2006.
87 "Pirated Films Hurt Production Capacity of Domestic Film Industry," China Legal News, 28 June 2006.
88 DVD vendors in conversation with the author. Yigao Shuma Market, Hangzhou, November 2006.
89 Statistical Yearbook of Hangzhou 2008.
90 Ibid, Research and Markets.
91 Ibid, Hong Kong Trade Development Council.

Published by Timezone 8 Limited
e-mail: info@timezone8.com
www.timezone8.com

ISBN 13: 978-988-18033-6-8

Editor/Author:
Mathieu Borysevicz

Contributions by Robert Venturi and Denise Scott Brown, Clarisa Diaz

Cover Design: Pamela Jue

Book Design:
Pamela Jue, Mathieu Borysevicz, Zhu Tao

Editorial Assistance:
Clarisa Diaz, Peter Borysevicz

Translations by:
Yang Yan, Mao Weidong, Fiona He

Chinese Editor:
Yang Yan, Azure Wu

All Principle Photography in this book by:
Mathieu Borysevicz

Additional Photography by:
Clarisa Diaz, He Kai, Liu Peng, Peng Yun, Maxine Wang, Wang Xiaofeng, Wei Lai

Second Printing in China, 2010

timezo..

明

Storefront for Art and Architecture
IBEX
LEARNING FROM HANGZHOU

Mikaku

序

我们应该首先称颂哪一样呢？是这本书丰富的内容，还是其中生机勃勃的图像？本书的内容深入探讨了中国当今城市丰富多彩的商业景象。照片在艺术上的造诣超乎寻常，描绘了这个新近出现的亚洲奇迹。

一系列多么奇妙的城市交响曲！在这座城市里，各种模式杂陈其间：传统的和现代的，渐进的和革命的，阳春白雪的和下里巴人的，市井的和商业的，中西合璧的和全球化的；建筑风格也是如此：中国传统风格、古典美术以及当代商业风格，这一切都创造了一个城市的蓬勃生机。

书里各种广告牌所占比重很大。多么有趣的牌子！电子图像与传统图像一搏高下，广告牌与涂鸦争夺领地，形成了一种无处不在的城市商业与社区媒介，以及这个时代不加掩饰的都市生活情趣。如果十七世纪的罗马是一座动感的空间之城，十九世纪的费城是一座充满活力的行业之城，二十世纪的芝加哥是一座充满生机的高楼之城，那么2008年的杭州可否就是一座动态交流之城？

照片的品质又给予本书另一个层面的内涵。细节的洞察力带着生动的美感，既具有预见性，又富于教育意义。这本书将会成为二十一世纪之初的《光辉城市》吗？我们认为如此。拉斯维加斯该让位了，让我们为杭州欢呼！为《向杭州学习》鼓掌致意——因为它展现了引人入胜的寻常景致，而寻常的景致却有可能是英雄式的壮美诗篇。

罗伯特•文丘里
丹尼斯•斯考特•布朗
2008年2月

PREFACE

Which should we proclaim first – the book's exuberant content or its exuberant illustrations? The content engages the rich commercial landscape of today's Chinese city. The photographs portray this burgeoning Asian phenomenon more artfully than any we've seen.

What a wonderful series of urban juxtapositions! In this city the coming together of life patterns – traditional and modern, evolutionary and revolutionary, high culture and vernacular, civic and commercial, Chinese-Eastern and global – and of architectural styles – classic Chinese, Classical Beaux Arts and contemporary commercial – create an urban dynamic that is supremely vital.

Here signs predominate. What signs! Electronic graphics vie with traditional graphics and billboards jostle graffiti to create a pervasive urban medium of commerce and community – and an urban joie de vivre unabashedly of our time. If 17th century Rome was the city of dynamic space, 19th century Philadelphia the city of dynamic industry, and 20th century Chicago the city of dynamic high-rise, is Hangzhou in 2008 the city of dynamic communication?

And the quality of the photography contributes another layer. Vividly aesthetic with a wicked eye for detail, it is also prescient and could be instructive. Will this book be the Ville Radieuse of the early 21st century? We think so. So move over Las Vegas and Viva Hangzhou! And Viva *Learning from Hangzhou* – for showing that the spectacular can be ordinary and the ordinary heroically spectacular.

Robert Venturi
Denise Scott Brown
February 2008

SHENG JIANHUA: HANGZHOU NOMAD by Clarisa Diaz